All Ears

All Ears

**Cultural Criticism,
Essays and Obituaries**

Dennis Cooper

Soft Skull Press

Some of these pieces have previously appeared in *Artforum,
Artscribe, Detour, George, Interview,* and *SPIN.*

Soft Skull Press thanks Billie Swift, Cat Tyc, Ira Silverberg
and Jessica (at *SPIN*) for their help.

www.softskull.com

for Craig Marks

INTRODUCTION

I'm a novelist who writes journalism, essays, and so on. That's how I think about it. Not to say I don't love writing nonfiction, and work hard, and care how it reads. But after writing everything from book reviews to feature articles for going on twenty years now, I still feel like someone who's wandered into a job I don't completely understand.

Basically, I think of these pieces as the result of a collaboration between particular editors, magazines, artists, and myself. I tend to be hired because of my fiction, seemingly in the hope that I can give some magazine a dose of my style and POV, and at the same time, fulfill its particular editorial interests. I wish I was more like the nonfiction writers I admire most—David Foster Wallace, Lester Bangs, Joan Didion, early Tom Wolfe, Gary Indiana, and others, who make every topic their own. But as someone who needs to rewrite sentences a hundred times before I'm satisfied with them, having short deadlines and preordained word counts forces me to rely on my editors' input, advice, and judgement. I find that process excitingly foreign, which is why I keep taking these jobs. Well, and because I get to hang out with people like Stephen Malkmus, Leonardo DiCaprio, Courtney Love and Keanu Reeves. And then, of course, there's the money.

Still, there are degrees of give and take. For instance, it took *SPIN* a year to run the piece "AIDS: Words from the Front," so I had time to fiddle the piece into something that seems entirely my own. On the other hand, my profile of Sonny Bono, originally published in *George,* had to rewritten so many times that it's almost unrecognizeable to me. Whether one is better than the other, I have no idea. "A Raver Runs Through It" was co-written with Joel Westendorf, an artist and musician who doesn't normally work with words, so that piece has it own curious quality.

As far as the other pieces go, you might or might not be interested to know that: (1) I was friends with Bob Mould when I wrote the feature on him for *SPIN*. There was a lot of pressure on him at that time to "come out," and, since he trusted me, we agreed I should be the guy to help him reveal his sexual preference in the way he saw fit. Unfortunately, there was a mix-up and the piece wasn't fact-checked with Mould before publication. He felt the article contained too much personal, friend-to-friend information, and he's barely spoken to me since. (2) To my knowledge, mine is the last in-depth interview Leonardo DiCaprio gave before *Titanic* turned him into a press-shy mega-star. Even at the time, he was wary of journalists, and I only got the gig because he knew my fiction, and had, for a brief, ill-advised moment, toyed with the idea of starring in the film version of my novel *Frisk*. (3) My Courtney Love feature hit the stands on the day Kurt Cobain killed himself, and I've always felt a little weird about comparing their marriage to Ozzie and Harriet's. But that really is how it seemed to me. (4) When I wrote "Too Cool for School," I was teaching in the Graduate Fine Arts Department at UCLA. Weirdly, the piece caused such a ruckus in the art world, and angered some of my fellow faculty members so much that, suffice to say, I no longer teach there. (5) Keanu Reeves' friendly joking, "No. [long pause] But ya never know," response to my question "Are you gay or what?" helped start a rumor that he was in fact gay that continues to this day. If it matters, he isn't, and was just being nice. (6) The Reeves interview, as well as the one with Stephen Malkmus, were truncated rather drastically when they were originally published. These are the original, full length versions.

I've worked with nothing but great editors: Craig Marks and Lee Smith (*SPIN*), Elizabeth Mitchell (*SPIN* and G*eorge*), Jack Bankwosky (*Artforum*), Judith Lewis (*The LA Weekly*), Matthew Collin (*Artscribe*), Graham Fuller (*Interview*), and Juan Morales (*Detour*). I'm really grateful to them. Lastly, I want to thank my friend and hero Sander Hicks, for letting me be a part of the mighty Soft Skull Press. Now see what you think.

– Dennis Cooper

AIDS: Words from the Front

(The names of the people in this article have been changed.)

I'm sitting at a table in the Onyx, a dimly lit East Hollywood coffee house decorated with clumsy neo-Expressionist paintings, and half full of book-reading trendoids. Jason, the client of an acquaintance who works with HIV-positive street kids, has agreed to share a couple of days of his endangered life if I promise to plug his band. They're called the Rambo Dolls, and more on them later. That's Jason storming through the entrance. I can just tell.

With his wild blond hair, bony face, huge blue eyes, and grunge garb—ripped jeans, Sandy Duncan's Eye T-shirt, untucked flannels, scuffed Docs—Jason looks like a rock star, specifically Soul Asylum's Dave Pirner. But once he joins me at my table, and I get a closer look, his face is almost scary, just a little too perfectly constructed. It's weird to think someone this conventionally cute could be homeless.

"How did you get infected?" I ask.

"Well, it was either from sharing needles with people I didn't know," he says, staring at his lap, "or from letting guys fuck me without a condom, or from fucking girls I knew had AIDS without a condom. I could've been infected a hundred times, you know?" He pauses, and his stare grows extremely forlorn. "Do you think that makes a difference?" He looks up at me for a second. "I mean, that I could've gotten infected a lot?"

I just sort of stammer that he should, like, be careful.

"Yeah, obviously! I mean I already should've been... more..." Suddenly he twists around in his chair, and yells toward the Onyx's door, "Go away! Do something!"

Every head turns. A scrawny young redheaded woman, maybe 26 years old, is standing outside on the sidewalk. "All right, all right," she yells back, and blurs out of sight to the right.

His...girlfriend?

Jason untwists. "Yeah," he says. "Katie. I'm crashing at her place right now. She's alright, she's just—she wants me to love her and I told her I can't because I'm going to die, but she still wants me to, so..." He cringes.

"That's a tough one."

He nods violently. "And she's a heroin junkie too," he continues, slumping down in his chair. "That's fucked-up because I'm off everything now since the HIV thing. So I have to watch her shoot up all the time and it's fucked. But I never liked heroin, so it's easier than if she was doing crystal or something I liked. But it makes her hard to deal with, you know?" He's growing increasingly hangdog, his gaze caught on what looks like a petrified muffin crumb on the table between us.

"I'm sure," I say. Anyway, what's this about his rock band?

"Oh, fuck." He tenses, kicks his chair back away from the table, and makes a face as if he has just been shot. "Now I have to live up to it, right? Maybe you should just come see us rehearse later, like I said. Then you can decide if..." He shrugs.

With such organizations as Covenant House, Angel's Flight, the Gay and Lesbian Center, and others, all concentrating their efforts on the plight of young runaways, you'd think the situation would be under control, to some degree at least. I did. Not according to Jason. But then he's made a point of avoiding, whenever humanly possible, every aspect of the available support services, though he can't really explain his aversion. He doesn't want to be "controlled," is the short and long of it. According to him, even the most religion-free outreach program has some sort of freedom-obliterating agenda. He prefers to have floating parental figures. In the past, he relied on a series of older men who paid him for sex and whose concern for his welfare was just authentic enough to provide a little comfort, just suspicious enough to be rejected guilt-free whenever he felt like it. Now he counts on his immediate friends, several of whom I will meet later this day, and all of whom seem to be what therapists call "caretaker types"—people devoted to Jason's well-being, often to a slightly hysterical degree. And, yeah, even in our brief contact, I distinctly feel an intense, father-and-son-ish psychological push-pull.

We're leaning on a parked car outside the Onyx. Half a block up the street, Katie keeps yoyo-ing in and out of a bookshop, neck craned, checking our status, I guess. I let Jason blab about whatever he wants. Mostly he rags on the Onyx clientele, and how, well, artsy-fartsiness is the opiate of the new bourgeoisie, basically. Classic punk stuff.

Jason may be an emotional wreck, but he's sharp, albeit in a knee-jerk, self-taught kind of way. For instance, his politics and musical tastes were formed by the brainy punk magazine Maximum RockNRoll, which he's been reading religiously since he was a kid. Now that we're in the daylight, I can see that he has a freshly shoplifted book by cultural theorist Noam Chomsky shoved between his belt and jeans. He's been meaning to dip into Chomsky since his pre-diagnosis, pre-homeless days, meaning four months ago.

Back then he lived with a bunch of other quasi-anarchistic teen squatters in an abandoned building just off Hollywood Boulevard. He'll talk about that year of his life in great detail, but the time before then—in other words, his entire childhood and adolescence—is off-limits. When he accidentally lets a detail slip—that he grew up in the San Fernando Valley, or that his father is a doctor, for instance—it's accompanied by a kind of physical explosion. The air is punched; the sidewalk stomped. When I press him, all Jason will admit about his past is that whatever happened, which is none of my business, it made him realize how people don't give a shit for each other, no matter what they say.

What about his friends?

"Right," Jason says. "Well, I don't keep them very long. Most of my friends aren't real friends, they're just guys who are into me sexually. But when they realize what an asshole I am, and that I'm never going to let them fuck me, they're gone."

Why doesn't he just let them fuck him? I mean, he's a hustler, so—

"Because they're my friends," he yells. Then he looks down at his scuffed-up Doc Martens, smiles, and clears his throat. "You're into me too, aren't you?"

"No," I say. And I'm not, actually.

Jason glances up. And his smile grows all weird and flirtatious. "Oh yeah, right," he mumbles.

I know that smile. My first boyfriend was a call boy, as were most of his friends. And in the days before AIDS, I used to hang around hustler bars, mostly because I liked the tension in the air. I've been given the hard sell by hustlers on hundreds of occasions, and Jason is obviously...well, if not an expert, then a veteran. Add that semi-expertise to his beauty, and he must do pretty well in that world. True?

"True," he agrees, and laughs uproariously. "But it's not like I'm spending my last days on earth in some rich scumbag's mansion." According to him, he's had innumerable chances to "sell out," as he puts it, particularly with "a famous record company executive," who he won't name, partially because the guy still rents him out on occasion and partially because he respects people's right to privacy. "But I guess if I was really considerate," he says, "I'd still be living in the squat and not with a fucking junkie." He shoots a murderous glare up the sidewalk. "Katie! Get your ass down here! Let's go!"

I'm driving Jason and Katie to her downtown apartment where the Rambo Dolls have arranged a rehearsal. At my request, Jason directs us along Hollywood Boulevard, pointing out haunts from his days in the squat. In a spot near Mann's Chinese Theater that he has just called "the world's greatest panhandling area," he sees one of his friends, a former squat-mate, now the lead singer in their band.

Bouncer is a tall, skinny, sweet-faced late teen with a long, floppy blond mohawk. He's accosting passersby with his hand out when Jason orders me over to the curb.

"Hey, shit sack!" Jason yells, shoving his head and shoulders through the open passenger window. He topples out onto the sidewalk. Bouncer helps him up, and they half-hug, half-wrestle for a few minutes, while tourists veer around them.

Katie and I watch from inside the car, trading bemused smiles. Assuming Jason is telling me the truth about her addiction, she's jonesing pretty badly. Her face is greenish white. Her pupils are gigantic. Her skinny arms are practically strangling her upper torso. "Jason's...such a...liar," she says, teeth chattering, watching the boys mock-battle.

"How so?"

"Like when he says he doesn't love me," she says. "I'm sure he told you that. But I put up with his bullshit. Nobody else ever did. He's a lot sicker than he says he is. You can't see it that much at first, but he's really underweight, and he has diarrhea all the time now. That's why he doesn't hustle very much anymore. So when—"

Suddenly Jason swings open the passenger door. He hurls himself inside, squashing Katie against me, and me against my door. Bouncer joins us, slamming the door shut behind him.

"Howdy," the new boy says.

"Two things. First, you can give Bouncer a ride, right?" Jason's face is about an inch from mine. I can smell AZT on his breath. It's kind of a sour chemical stink that doesn't fit with his being at all. "And, okay, secondly he wants to know it, after you drop me and Katie off, you feel like fucking him for not very much money at all. Then you guys can meet us at Katie's later for the rehearsal. Because I told him you're a..." Jason's eyes get confused. "queer? Is that what you guys want to be called now? Because he's queer too, and he's a nice guy, and he's broke, right?"

After we drop off Jason and Katie, I buy Bouncer a meal, and he tells me his story, which is as heavily censored as Jason's. As for the present, he mostly panhandles, smokes a lot of pot, and hustles occasionally on Santa Monica Boulevard, although hustling depresses him, maybe because he's queer and expects too much affection from his johns or something. Unlike Jason, he's happy to utilize support organizations for runaways when need be. To him, it's worth a little lecturing and "group encounter bullshit" to sleep in a warm bed. At the time of our conversation, he was still commandeering a room in the Hollywood squat where Jason used to live. After lunch, he walks me there.

We enter a faded Victorian mansion that has clearly been through several subsequent lives as an apartment building. Its fanciness is so smashed and dirtied that it looks like a baroque cave. Most of the squatters are away at the moment, hanging out on the boulevard, panhandling for fast food and drug cash, but there's a young heterosexual couple, maybe 14 years old, playing cards in the former mansion's large, bare, filthy living room. They have angelic faces, dated punk haircuts, wear several layers of threadbare clothes, and I can smell their body odor all the way up to the second floor, where Bouncer is showing me his bedroom, a former walk-in closet: mattress, tangled blanket, small hill of clothing. He plops down in the middle, rests his eyes on his own crotch for a second, then looks up at me and smiles. One of those smiles.

"So who gets to live in the squat?" I ask.

"Anybody," he says. "You just have to be honest, and not too strung out. And you can't fuck around with our stuff."

"I take it Jason broke the rules."

"Every one of them. I fought for him. And we almost let him stay, because he's so fucking beautiful."

"**M**y mind works like this," Jason is saying. We're standing in the narrow hallway outside Katie's apartment. She's inside, shooting up. Bouncer is at the corner store stealing us a six pack. "Usually I don't think about having AIDS. I mean about having HIV. I always forget that it's not technically AIDS yet. But then when I do remember, this is what happens: It's usually right after I've had sex with somebody, not Katie so much, but with men who pay me. I think, 'I have HIV, okay, but it'll be fine.' The doctor says I have maybe ten years from the time I got infected before I die if I take care of myself. But then I think, 'Well, I could've gotten infected seven years ago, because I've been letting guys fuck me since I was 12, as weird as that sounds. Then I think how many drugs I've done, and what that's probably done to my immune system. And I start to get really scared, and I think, 'Fuck it. I'm going to kill myself now before I get sick.' Because it's too much, you know? Then I think, 'I hate everybody. Somebody gave this to me. You can't trust anyone.' And I get so tense that I want to kill people, and my friends get shit from me because they're there. And then I get really guilty about treating my friends shitty, so I apologize to them and they're usually okay about it. And that's a relief. So I feel better and I've sort of forgotten about the AIDS. So my mind's made this weird journey to get me away from thinking I have AIDS, I mean HIV. Do you think it does that consciously?"

Jason always asks these impossible questions. Luckily his attention span sucks, and he immediately turns to Katie's door, pounding, "Wake up, you fucking pincush-ion!"

Minutes later, the rest of the Rambo Dolls show up. Brian is a tall, polite African-American in his early 20s. Six months ago, a friend bought him an hour with Jason as a joke birthday gift, and the two became friends. A bass player, he's the only member of the band with even a smidgen of technical prowess. Bart, guitarist, is a hippie-esque 16-year-old, newly off drugs and a born-again Christian. He doesn't say much. He's brought along a crappy little amp into which he and Brian both plug their instruments. Jason, the drummer, can't afford a kit, so he perches on the edge of Katie's bed with a coffee-table art book in his lap and an unsharpened pencil in each fist.

Over the next, oh, hour and a half, Jason thwacks the book's covers so violently that he manages to spar with the general din. As much as I can tell from the Rambo Dolls' lurching sketch of a sound, the music is a parochial variation on hardcore. Sort of like if the Shaggs had grown up listening to the Melvins maybe. Bouncer, pogoing around mid-room with a humongous grin, sings/yells some artsy-fartsy lyrics that evince standard punky politics regarding racism, drug use, misogyny, etc. Watching these Little Rascal-style antics, I feel kind of sad, truth be told. Fortunately the boys are oblivious. It's only after Bart and Brian have left, and Bouncer is napping in a corner, that Jason nervously asks me what I think, by which time I'm mentally prepared to lie a little, offer encouragement. "Very cool," I say.

"Thanks," Jason says happily. Katie's sprawled in his lap, nodding out. "Yeah, I think in a year we'll be famous. That's my goal."

"How famous?"

"As famous as...and as good as...Sandy Duncan's Eye."

"But they're not very famous," I say. I'm beginning to see what Katie means. In the sharp window light, Jason's body does seem sort of underinflated, his facial skin bunched a little too tightly around the bones.

"They're famous enough," he says.

"Why not as famous as U2?"

Jason goggles at me. "Because they suck."

"Okay, but why not be in a great band that happens to be really famous?"

He looks horrified. "Impossible, man."

"Then what else? Other life goals, I mean."

"To not die. Not for a long time." He glances at Katie, then smiles conspiratorially at me. "And...have a great girl-friend," he half-whispers, then checks to see if she's awake. Nope. "And be rich...somehow." Now he's crowing again. "And never see my parents again. Uh...be a great drummer."

"Like who?"

"Adam Pfahler."

"Who's in..."

"Jawbreaker. Fuck, they're great. Okay, I want my band to be as famous as Jawbreaker. And as good as them."

"Jawbreaker's more famous than Sandy Duncan's Eye?"

"Well, Jawbreaker's known for being so brilliant. Sandy Duncan's Eye is more known for their weird name. So it would be better to be like Jawbreaker. " And he shoots me a grin that makes him look about seven years old. Suddenly it decays into a grimace, and he punches the air. "But I'm going to die soon anyway, so...who cares!" He glares into space for a second, then shoves Katie off of him. She hits the floor, thwack, not too far away from Bouncer, rolls slowly onto her side, and winces up at Jason with this deep if very foggy concern.

"Shit," she slurs," are you...crying, Jason?"

And, yeah, fuck, he is.

Fast-forward. This day with Jason was supposed to be the first of a handful of visits, but, soon thereafter, he just sort of disappeared. I called Katie's to set up a meeting, and she screamed at me that she didn't know or care where he was. My friend, the part-time counselor who'd led me to Jason, hadn't seen him in months. He had a dozen other kids to worry about. It took quite a few drives up and down Hollywood Boulevard to locate the panhandling Bouncer. He said he hadn't heard from Jason either, and was worried, not that his friend was in trouble, but that Jason had gone home to his parents' house rather than staying with his "real family"—his friends. It wasn't many days later that L.A. had its earthquake. It severely damaged the squat building, whose inhabitants, including Bouncer, scattered to who-knows-where.

To this day, I'll go out of my way to drive down Santa Monica Boulevard's hustler strip, looking for Jason's silhouette. Not that I know what I'd say to him. Get some help, blah blah blah. Maybe six months ago I ran into Brian, bassist of the now-defunct Rambo Dolls, at a club. Yeah, he said, Jason was still missing. He just shrugged, but his eyes looked pretty distraught. Maybe, he said, some beautiful rich woman had taken Jason in. Right. This is a world where people come and go, and you rarely learn why or how. You have to use your imagination. You love your friends and lovers intensely, but you're always prepared to shut down. Maybe Jason really did luck out. Who's to know? But is it wrong to half-hope that he went home after all? Because I half-do. Because, as physically destructive as that setup might be, at least it's real. It would mean Jason was somewhere, not nowhere. But then it's easy for me to say since I don't even know him.

Flashback. Post-rehearsal. I'm driving Jason and Bouncer to the hustler strip, where they've decided to spend the night earning some quick cash. Jason's freaked out, ranting, mostly about whether or not he's going to tell the men who buy him that he has AIDS. I've been trying to convince him that not telling would be sort of evil. Bouncer has been mumbling his agreement with me. The more I argue, the more extreme Jason's opinions become, which makes me wonder if his obnoxiousness isn't just some kind of self-hating yowl for sympathy. Anyway, the atmosphere in the car is really confused. It's getting dark, so the sidewalks are starting to fill with teenage male loiterers, mostly shirtless, their eyes scanning each passing windshield. We've stopped at a light just west of LaBrea. Without a word, Jason reaches across Bouncer, opens the passenger door, pushes his friend outside, then basically steps over him and stomps out of sight. After a second, Bouncer struggles to his feet, closes my car door, and leans way in through the window, shooting me what I guess is an apologetic grin, although it's so full of worry and confusion that I don't know how to respond. So maybe I seem worried too, I can't tell. And maybe that's why Bouncer bends over close enough to me that I can smell his breath, which is as thick with AZT as Jason's. "We'll be okay," he says, and kisses my cheek. Then he withdraws, and chases his friend into...wherever.

KEANU REEVES INTERVIEW

Equal parts sex symbol, madman, oaf, and over-grown kid, Keanu Reeves is unique among younger actors in his ability to fill movies with a specific, contentious energy, no matter how small his role. His is a presence that lies somewhere between Crispin Glover's manic self-involvement and Jimmy Stewart's gentle remove, with maybe a dash of Jacques Tati tossed in. Reeves—a walking explosion of misbehaved limbs—would have been great in the silent film era. In his bigger roles—especially in flawed movies like *Permanent Record, Prince of Pennsylvania,* and *I Love You to Death*—he's capable of literally wrenching plots loose from their flimsy foundations when need be, making them tag along after his characters' wild quests for sensation. In his best movies, *River's Edge, Bill and Ted's Excellent Adventure,* and *Dangerous Liaisons,* he seems to embody the sensitive soul of all disenfranchised youth. Two upcoming projects match him with suitably maverick directors, Kathryn Bigelow's *Riders on the Storm,* [ultimately released as *Point Break*] and, especially, Gus Van Sant's *My Own Private Idaho.* His next movie in release will be *Aunt Julia and the Scriptwriter* [ultimately released as *Tune in Tomorrow...*] later this year. I met with the tanned, newly muscular Reeves at one of his occasional hangouts, Linda's, a restaurant-cum-jazz-club located in the nether reaches of the Melrose strip.

DENNIS COOPER: Is it true you're playing a male prostitute in Gus Van Sant's new film?
KEANU REEVES: Yeah, I play Scottie, who's based

on...Hal? Prince Hal? From, um—Shakespeare. I come from a wealthy background and I've denied that. And I've been on the streets for three years.

"The streets" meaning Santa Monica Boulevard?

Yeah, yeah. But in Seattle. It's not quite au courant. It's more about family. I call it, "Where's Dad?" Hopefully River Phoenix will be doing it with me. And if that happens, then who knows what's going to happen.

You'd both be prostitutes?

Yeah!

What a funny idea.

Yes. He plays a character called Mike, who has an extreme case of narcolepsy. So he'll pass out and awaken and the film follows him around. I'm more like a side character.

Sounds cool. Any relationship between this and "Wolfboy," that gay play you did in Toronto early on in your career?

[laughing] Um—wow. No. The guy that I played in "Wolfboy" was a jock, who just lost it. He was under so much pressure, he didn't know what was goin' on. Then he fell in love with this guy who gave him back his sense of power. And even then I dumped the guy [chuckling]. And he killed me. Cut me.

Yeah, I heard.

He sucked my blood.

Friends of mine in Toronto sent me some yellowed clippings.

Really? What did they—I don't recall.

Oh, um—just that it was disgusting. The play was revolting, et cetera.

Oh, yeah!

And there should never have been anything like it perpetrated on a stage.

Really! Well, that's kind of cool. The poster was the cast in white T-shirts, kind of wetted down. I had my eyes closed and this guy is almost kissing me with this like grin? So the first couple of performances, we had leather boys comin' out. You know, caps and the whole deal. And they were walking out at intermission because there weren't enough shoes flying.

You grew up in Toronto. Wildly, innocently?

When I see stuff in LA now I realize how safe and sheltered my upbringing was. We didn't even do graffiti, you know? We'd build go-karts called "Fireball 500." I mean we did sling chestnuts at teachers' heads, and in grade 8 hash started to come around, and LSD kinda. But Toronto's become like a shopping center now. Under all those banks you can actually go shopping 14 city blocks underground. You can buy lotto tickets every 500 feet.

In Tokyo they're about to begin construction on these 60-story underground buildings. Combination apartment complex, shopping mall, business office.

Wow! Do they have floors or are they gonna be like spirals going down or something?

I saw computer-animated mock-ups of them on CNN. They look like silos connected by a futuristic subway system. The point is, you'll never have to leave them. There'll be parks, museums—

What kind of light?

The Japanese have figured out a way to reflect light down via a series of mirrors or something, so that its quality is better then direct sunlight. Sounds a little suspicious to me. But the die is cast.

Who knows what the human beast is gonna do under there!

You play bass guitar, right?

Do I play it? You know, it's all relative.

You're not starting a band à la River Phoenix?

Um—I wouldn't mind doing bar band shit, I guess.

What kind of music do you listen to?

OK, where to begin, where to begin. Let's see, Hüsker Dü, Joy Division...The Ramones changed my life. Oh, and what's that band? It's like an industrial band.

British, or Canadian, or—

American. Black—Black—Big Black.

Oh, they're great! Do you know their song "Kerosene," about these kids who are so bored they light each other on fire just to have something to do? Someone should buy the film rights to that song. Maybe you?

Yeah. Who else do I like? There's the Pixies, but I mean I don't know if I love 'em. I was telling some guy in a frat in San Diego what bands I like and he says, "Oh, so you like slightly alternative music." [laughing]

Were you into punk when it started? I guess you must have been pretty young.

I'm like second-circle punk. But yeah, man!! [clapping] Totally!! GBH and the Exploited are my two hardcore bands of choice. I love playing them too.

Actually, I've always thought there was something very punk about your acting, not only your erratic energy, but the way you seem incapable of conveying dishonesty, no matter who you're playing. Which I guess is why you have this punk cult following.

Oh yeah. King Punk.

No, really. For instance I know these punks in Toronto who adore you so much that they invented a dance called "The Keanu Stomp" based on the way you walked in *Prince of Pennsylvania*.

No!!!

Yeah. Apparently it's turning into a bit of a fad. There are slam pits full of punks doing "The Keanu Stomp" even as we speak. In fact two of these punks, Bruce La Bruce and Candy, who head up this gay and lesbian anarchist group called the New Lavender Panthers, begged me to ask you some questions for them. Is that ok?

The New Lavender Panthers! Whoa!! Sure, it's okay.

Alright—"Why haven't you made a movie with Drew Barrymore yet?"

Oh ho ho! They're not up on their Keanu lore because I did work with Drew on a Xmas TV special. This was after she got off drugs.

"Was Rob Lowe gross to work with on *Youngblood?"*
What?! No, Rob's okay.

"Why haven't you worked with Molly Ringwald yet?"
I want to! I want to! I want to!

"Would you rather be murdered by John Wayne Gacy, Richard Speck, Martha Beck or Gertrude Baniszewski?"
I don't know what their specialties were?

Gacy molested and tortured teenage boys. Speck raped and killed nurses. I forget what the others did.
Hard to decide, man.

"Any inside info on the two Coreys?"
Hm. I know exactly how much heroin Corey Feldman was arrested with to the decimal point!

"Why haven't you made a European art film yet? (Might we suggest Dario Argento, Michelangelo Antonioni, or Lothar Lambert?)"
Oh, yeah. I'll just send them a tape of me going, "Whoa! Bodacious!" Sure.

And finally, "Are you gay or what?" Come on, make it official.
No. [long pause] But ya never know.

Cool. So are you a very politically aware person?
No, I'm an ignorant pig. I'm makin' movies in Hollywood, you know? The things that I'm doing are pretty sheltered. For me, with acting and the parts and all, it's very self-involved, especially between projects. Once you get a part, you're liberated. You can find out what that character thinks.

Your character in *Parenthood* was kind of weird politically.
Yeeesss?

Well, initially he was an outsider in every way. He even had a different energy level than anyone else in the movie. But by the end he's happily ensconced in that big family portrait with all the other characters, holding a newborn infant.

Yeah. I dug that guy, man. He was trying.

Well, at one point your character does this monologue about how his father used to wake him up by flicking lit cigarettes at his head. It concluded with a statement that could be interpreted as vaguely homophobic.

Really! Like what?

He says, "They'll let any butt-reaming asshole be a father these days," which seems to imply that "father" is some kind of godlike state, and "butt-reaming asshole" i.e., gay male, isn't.

Oh, that is homophobic. It's weird.

Your character does this fantastic doubletake right after that. Some friends of mine interpreted that as you trying to express your discomfort as an actor at having to say that line.

Right. Yeah. "Butt-reaming asshole" was a weird line. But no. The character's just dismissing his past. He understands it, he's beyond it, it was ugly and he doesn't want any part of it. That doubletake's like him going: Fuck that shit.

Do you want to have a family?

Yeah.

Do you have a serious girlfriend?

Um—not—not that heavy. I want kids.

How many?

Three.

What sexes?

Whatever comes out.

Do you read much? Books, I mean.

How about if I said I don't read as much as I'd like to.

Nothing recently?

Um—yeah. I've been rereading *Letters to a Young Poet* and *The Autobiography of Malcolm X*. And some John Rechy novels as research for the Gus Van Sant film. Oh I love Philip K. Dick.

Me too. I just saw *Total Recall*.

How is it?

Disappointing. Everything's in the trailer. The K. Dick story it's based on gets avalanched about an hour in. Then it just turns into an excuse to blow $70 million. Explosion movie.

Yeah.

Have you read Dick's short stories? He'd begin writing by having like a fantasy, like—he would take a glass and go, "Hm, that's ironic." And write a story, you know?

Well, he was on speed all the time.

I want to be on speed! I've never been on speed. I want to be a speed freak for a while.

It's really—

Is that a stupid thing to say?

No, no. I love speed. I mean I used to do speed all the time. Trouble is, you do get really depressed for three days afterwards.

It burns you out?

Yeah. It's ultimately not worth it. I used to do crystal meth, which is scary. I'd snort it.

Yummmm! Wild!!!

I know. It's yum indeed. Speaking of speed, you do a lot of films. Do you like it that way?

Yeah, definitely. Like recently *Aunt Julia and the Scriptwriter* has been having reshoots. In between them I did a couple of parts in student films.

Didn't you do a Shakespeare play in Massachusetts last year?

Yeah, *The Tempest.* Played Trinculo, and it was a blast. Andre Gregory played Prospero. His daughter Marina played Miranda.

Gregory must be intense.

He was v*ery* intense. Anyway, my next half a year is pretty much set. With Gus Van Sant, and I'm doing *Bill and Ted's Excellent Adventure, Part 2*, or *Bill and Ted Go to Hell*, or *Bill and Ted's Bogus Journey.* We're also doing a *Bill and Ted* Saturday morning cartoon, and that's kind of trippy. And *Riders on the Storm* with Kathryn Bigelow.

Based on the Doors song of the same name?

No, or—I don't think so. I play an FBI agent who has to infiltrate some surfers who are bank robbers. The character is a kind of adrenaline junkie, and there's this other adrenaline junkie, and they push each other into jumping out of airplanes, shooting guns, shit like that.

Is he a classic Keanu Reeves-ian character—sweet, confused, distracted, awkward?

I call it victim acting.

Do you make a point of seeking out roles like that?

Well, I don't know about manifest destiny and all. You get what you put out and all that shit? I guess it's just been my lot so far.

Even your creepy characters are so sympathetic. In *I Love You to Death* you were supposed to be a thief, but—

No, my guy was just harmless. Larry Kasdan wanted this guy to be beat up by the world. Just kind of in a daze. Harmless and drugged. So they hired me. [laughing]

That daze is one of the things I really love about what you do. You're always kind of talking around what you actually want to say.

Right, right.

Most actors just manufacture emotion and expect audiences to match it. With your characters, it's their inability to produce that's the key. They're often, if not perpetually, distressed, spooked, weirded-out by the world. They're always fighting with their contexts.

Always, man! Always.

Granted most of them are teenagers, but they're not exactly future stockbrokers, which seems like the teen norm nowadays.

No, not at all. Actually, the futures of most of my characters are pretty bleak [laughing]. You know, Matt, Ted, Rupert—who knows what they're gonna do.

Do you research your characters?

Definitely. Definitely. Right now with this film *Riders on the*

Storm I've been hanging out with athletes, FBI agents, police, people in college fraternities. I'm seein' a whole other part of the world, you know? When I did Ted I took stuff from cartoons. Stuff comes up that you never thought of. I look for physical things, background, and emotionally where he's at for every second. I'm pretty flexible. I've studied some of the Uta Hagen techniques and Stanislavsky, and I've done some—you know, some basic physical Grotowski exercises, and I've read some Artaud. A lot of times you get tired, 'cause you're 17 and you got a certain kind of energy that they dig. You know? In some of the character stuff, I've got a chance to explore more, working with a whole new caliber of people like Stephen Frears, Tim Hunter. *River's Edge!* That's a movie, man. American cinema!

Yeah, a great movie. I keep waiting for Tim Hunter to do another movie. It's been years now. I guess he did a *Twin Peaks*.

He did? Did you see it?

Yeah.

What was it like?

It was nice. It was sparer than the others. Not quite as surrealistic. So, where do you think you fit into the Brat Pack, if at all?

The *Brat* Pack? I have nothing to do with them.

Do you think your acting style's fundamentally different from theirs?

Jeesh! What?! *No!!!* Agggghhh! I really respect those guys, man. Emilio Estevez, Judd Nelson, Kiefer, Rob Lowe, all those guys. They've really set a path for us. Who would have thought that you'd give a development deal to a 23-year-old actor?

Well, unlike them, you don't seem like a career-socializer. I never see your mug in *Details, Vanity Fair,* et cetera.

Right. I guess 'cause I'm a nerd.

You don't avoid trendy photo ops?

No, I dig going out, but—you know, I have *fun.* I don't get many invitations and stuff—it's just kind of whatever happens. Once in a while I'll ask my friends, "What're you doing? Where are you going? What's going on?" I'll go see art, I'll do whatever—buy a drink, dance, play. All that shit. Sometimes I go to clubs. I dig the blues, man. The blues have always had some of the *best* times, *best* feelings I've ever had. The last person I saw was Buddy Guy, but it was in a bad space. Just bummed me out. Everyone was sittin' down, and they had candles in the middle of the tables! So it's like, "Bababawawa!" [he mimes a frenetic guitar player] And everyone's like [claps politely], "Excellent music."

Do your friends tend to be actors?

Some of 'em. Yeah. Alex Winter, John Cullan, Dean Feiffer. Alan Boyce I don't see much of, but I love his guts.

It must be weird making films, seeing a smallish group of people constantly for four or five months, then never seeing them again.

Yeah, right. "Howya doin', man?" "Bye." "Good to see you at the Academy Awards."

Do you want to say something about your motorcycle? I saw it parked out front.

My motorcycle. My 1974, 850 Norton Commando, high-performance English touring motorcycle. Yaaggghhhhhh!!!

Didn't you have a semi-serious accident?

I've fucked up a couple of times.

I thought so. When you took your shirt off in *Prince of Pennsylvania* you had this porcelain upper body. But when you had your shirt off in *Parenthood,* it looked all gnarly.

[laughing] I love that bike, man.

Well, not to be too parental or anything, but don't kill yourself. You've got a pretty lovestruck cult of fans to think about. And you're getting more and more famous. I mean that's—

Yeah, I'm pseudo-quasi.

Pseudo-quasi-famous?

Pseudo-quasi. Yeah. I mean, why is *Interview* even doing this?

I asked to. I think you're one of those guys who's like— they don't think of you until someone suggests it, then they go, "Of course!"

Right, right. I'm not really around. I'm around Yeah.

So where *are* you, if you know what I mean?

Um—lately?

Okay.

Lately. Training, surfing. On the weekends I've been kind of cruising the boulevards. LA is so trippy. Chhww. It becomes like a small town really quick. On those weekend nights the prostitutes are out, and the kids from school, and people cruising, and in the clubs all that stuff is going on? I ride my bike sometimes. I'll just go out, say, around one? Midnight? And I'll ride until four? Goin' through the city to see who's doin' what where, you know? Going downtown, riding around and just—I care, you know?

About—

Yeah. Just to look around. Great.

Love Conquers All

Our story begins where it ends, at 5 AM, in a parking lot in Seattle's warehouse district. Hole is huddled together against the side of some huge delivery truck, forcing expressions at once eager and snarly on to their spaced-out faces, while a photographer snap, snap, snaps. For most of the night, guitarist Eric Erlandson, drummer Patty Schemel, and bassist Kristen Pfaff, a.k.a. Hole's lesser known three-fourths, have been inside a photo studio's office area, hypnotized by a crappy TV, flipping aimlessly between infotainment and the late, late news. Meanwhile, their leader, an elaborately lit and costumed Courtney Love, is in the next room vamping her way through what seems like a hundred rolls of film. Occasionally, she rushes in, changes clothes, then rushes out, joking guiltily with her cohorts. "You'd better behave yourselves," she announces with a motherly chirp.

Love is a curious superstar. She's amazing looking, even weirdly gorgeous: fit, paler than pale, her features both soft and blunt, with a big wad of lipsticked lips, and huge, perpetually startled blue eyes capable of great ferocity. But she lacks the spartan androgyny required of '90s sex symbols. With her soft, recently slimmed waist, big bones, and shock-tactical makeup, she seems slightly out of date, more a time-traveling silent film siren than any kind of direct competition for Kate Moss or Winona Ryder. Watching her strike the prerequisite "bad girl" poses for the photographer, I can't help wondering if this hellishly beautiful, punk-derived image—an image she has carefully maintained with some refinements since her career's earliest beginnings—honestly suits the woman.

The previous afternoon, dressed in a simple blouse

and slacks, roots showing, talking animatedly about her life, her band, and its new album, *Live Through This*. Love had reminded me a bit of the late, great Simone de Beauvoir. Like de Beauvoir, Love is very intelligent, kind of workaholic, and full of curious, knowledgeable takes on her culture. She's also inherently charismatic, albeit in a strange, almost "anti-"way. So while this public image—the vengeful female—may be useful to Love as a feminist tool, it simplifies her as well, coloring her natural sensuality into something wacky. I've seen people point at her picture, then roll their eyes and lick their lips, like she was some comic-book character with big tits, the punk-rock Cyndi Lauper. But if Love is a cartoon, then she's drawn more in the style of Peter Bagge's fiercely bratty Girly Girl than Betty or Veronica. Who else but Love would have the smarts and audacity, after the horrific accusations leveled against her maternal qualifications, to write a song about her tabloid pregnancy featuring the barbed lines "And I don't do the dishes/I throw them in the crib"?

Let's get this out of the way. When Love talks about husband Kurt Cobain, which she does with some frequency, it's with affection and slight amusement. Mostly he shows up in benign little anecdotes. Like how she keeps finding him dolled up in women's sweaters from the '50s. Or how, at her urging, he recently agreed to buy them a Lexus. But, after one relatively brief spin around town, and the catcalls of virtually all of their old friends, Cobain insisted they take it back. So they did. Now they're back to his scuzzy old Valiant. If you only knew Cobain by Love's descriptions, you'd think he was an adorable, antic-prone young lug, more Ozzie Nelson than Ozzy Osbourne. And maybe that's exactly who he is. Point is, her love for him, and for their daughter Frances Bean, is obvious.

I'd been forewarned by Geffen's publicist, by friends of hers, even by the rest of Hole, that Courtney Love doesn't trust journalists. Not since *Vanity Fair*'s Lynn

Hirschberg, whose infamous 1992 profile portrayed Love as little more than Cobain's heroin-addicted, gold-digging girlfriend. The article contained a particularly scandalous quote, attributed to a "business associate." "Courtney was pregnant and she was shooting up," it said. What followed was an approximately yearlong trashing of the couple, chronicled rather exhaustively in Michael Azzerad's Nirvana bio, *Come As You Are.*

"Yeah, Lynn," Love sighs when the subject is broached. "I did a little private investigating on her, you know, and she has no friends. None. None!" For the next, oh, 40 minutes or so, Love's conversation keeps veering back to Hirschberg, usually with disclaimers. As much as she may wish Hirschberg dead, Love admits she continues to read *Vanity Fair.* "Shit," she says at the end of one particularly lengthy diatribe. "Why can't I just fucking shut up about the bitch? Okay, that's it. Zip." She raises one hand and makes a slash across her lips. (When asked to comment, Hirschberg laughed and said, "I thought Courtney was my friend.")

So what about the actual charges? "Innocent," Love says, smiling mysteriously. "Isn't that obvious?" Okay, how about claims that you punched out four people last year, including K records-Beat Happening's Calvin Johnson, British wrier Victoria Clarke, and a young female Nirvana fan who called her "Courtney Whore" in a Seattle 7-Eleven? "There's a lot more to those stories, but I don't intend to go into it." Several journalists told me they'd received threatening phone messages after criticizing her in print. "So?" When I mention Cobain's interest in guns, she cuts me off with a glower. Bringing up last year's legal battle to keep custody of Frances Bean (a result of the *Vanity Fair* drug inferences) only magnifies the glower. On a lighter note, Lydia Lunch recently accused Love of ripping off her persona. "That's too bad, because I admire her a lot." Well, how about the fact that I lot of people just think you're a mean, horrible person?

"Look," Love says. "Years ago in a certain town, my reputation had gotten so bad that every time I went to a party, I was expected to burn the place down and knock out every window. So I would go into social situations and try my best to be really graceful and quiet and aloof. But sometimes when people are bearing down on you so hard, and want you to behave in a certain way, you just do it because you know you can.

"I'm so busy these days pleading with everyone that I'm lucid, that I'm educated, that I'm middle-class," she continues. "It's stupid. If you ask me, why aren't people on the cases of the real assholes of this world, like Axl Rose and Steve Albini, both of whom should be exterminated. Really, they should leave on a shuttle to the sun. They shouldn't be on the earth. Because they're not good for anything."

I'd been told by a mutual friend that Love tends to feel comfortable around gay men "as long as they don't like disco." Hoping to warm up the atmosphere a little, I drop the names of a few famous actors I bedded when younger, and sure enough she giddily spills some beans herself. She practically begs me to "out" a notoriously homophobic music producer. Sorry. We move on. She has a few less-than-flattering adjectives for Evan Dando's physique. "I'm the one that got him to stop taking off his shirt all the time," she says. Then there's the sad tale of her arch-enemy Axl Rose's rapidly receding hairline, and his crazed search for a cure. "That's what happens when you mix Prozac and heroin." Finally, she regales me with a long, hilarious story about how Eddie Van Halen showed up backstage at a recent Nirvana show and practically begged to join them onstage for the encore, completely oblivious to the fact that bands like Nirvana exist partly to destroy dinosaurs like himself.

"I was talking to Sophie Mueller, the director of our new video," Love says. It's a few minutes later. She's chummier now, curled up in her chair, gazing contentedly out a tinted hotel window at Seattle's ugly harbor. "And she asked, 'What do you want to project?' Well, it's kind of pompous to do this, but I thought, 'What is my public image?' I kind of assessed my character flaws, and what I need to work on, what's good and bad about me, what my unknown qualities are. And...it's so hard to know.

"Because there are people like this journalist who interviewed us one night. He really believed that I was like him. You know, that I grew up in a trailer park, that I'm a drunk full of incest stories. I kept trying to calm him down. And the only thing that shut him up was when I read his astrological chart out loud, and even then he was hanging all over me, drooling. It was like being stuck in a room with a drunk Rupert Pupkin [the pathetic stand-up comedian portrayed by Robert De Niro in *The King of Comedy*]. And I love Rupert Pupkin. There's a Rupert Pupkin in all of us, but I killed mine a long time ago. And that guy should too."

A long time ago may or may not mean Eugene, Oregon, where Love grew up the bookish, overweight kid of well-educated, upper-middle-class parents. She doesn't really like to talk about them, but from what slips out, you don't get the feeling that they were or are particularly monstrous. Mom's a "New Age therapist," as Love describes her. In fact, Linda Carol is a respected psychologist, whose celebrity clients include '60s radical-turned-jailbird Katherine Anne Power. The name Hole is partly inspired by a saying of her mother's: "You can't walk around with a big hole inside yourself." (It's also inspired by a line in Euripides's *Medea:* "There's a hole that pierces right through me.") Love is no longer in contact with her father, Hank Harrison, author of *The Dead: A Social History of the Haight-Ashbury Experience,* and would only say of him that his single claim to fame was his long-ago, peripheral involvement with the Grateful Dead. Harrison's ties with the Dead were tight enough, however, that you can find a young Courtney Love in the extended family group photo on the back of *Aoxomoxoa,* the Dead's third LP.

Eugene is a university town, woodsy, relatively unfucked-over by gentrification, with decent book and CD stores. Nevertheless, it's a dullish place if your ambitions are huge and culturally based like Love's were. So, after suffering through the usual peer shit that befalls rebellious smarties, she took off. From her contacts in nearby Portland, she went to work informally for Bob Pitchland, a street person raconteur who's become quasi-famous as Gus Van Sant's model for one of the central characters in *My Own Private Idaho.* Under Pitchland's auspices, and with off-and-on financial support from her folks, she traveled the world, living for brief periods in such places as Taiwan and Tokyo, and taking care of her mentor's spurious business.

In the early '80s, she settled in Liverpool for a couple of years, attending school and making her first serious contact with the world of rock stars. As an adolescent, Love had adored sensitive singer-poet types such as Joni Mitchell, Laura Nyro and Leonard Cohen, while taking note of the condescending way they were portrayed by the rock press, "like ethereal little fairies." Now she fell for equally poetic but noisier bands like Echo and the Bunnymen and the Teardrop Explodes. She worshiped Bunnymen frontman Ian McCulloch and claims to have copped most of her stage moves from him. When she wasn't in class, she followed his band around England. "I ran into Ian again not too long ago at this hotel," she says. "He walked in dressed in his tennis whites, and, you know, he'd aged a lot, like great beauties do. And he saw me and he gave me this look like, 'What the fuck are *you* doing here?' He didn't like me at all."

Through Love's connections in the British rock scene, she met film director Alex Cox, who was revered at the time for the punkish cult film *Repo Man.* Cox came very close to casting her as the lead in *Sid and Nancy,* the project he was then developing around Nancy Spungen's mother's memoir, *And I Don't Want to Live This Life.* Luckily for Love, she lost the part to Chloe Webb, winding up instead with a tiny role as one of Nancy's bereaved friends. "Can you imagine?" she says, shaking her head at the thought of living down that particular portrayal on her résumé. But at the time she was crestfallen. Fighting suicidal depression, she signed on with a small acting/modeling agency, and wound up working as a stripper in the Far East for the next year or so. "Stripping's alright," she says. "It's better than prostitution. I was lucky, because I was fat. So nobody paid attention to me."

It was in the late '80s that Love met one of her closest friends, Los Angeles artist Joe Mama, who says, "She was the same then as now. She had this attitude like 'I'm a freak, but I know what I'm doing.' It wasn't calculating, it was scary." He remembers that she moved around a lot, living for brief periods in LA, San Francisco, and Minneapolis. It was in Minneapolis that, along with Kat Bjelland and L7's Jennifer Finch, she formed an early version of Babes in Toyland, described by one friend as sounding like an "atonal Roches." For maybe a week she was a member of Faith No More, and remains friendly with the band's Roddy Bottum. One night she met guitarist and begrudging Capitol Records' employee Eric Erlandson. They hit it off, started to pal around, and eventually, with the help of a classified ad in *Flipside,* scraped together the first incarnation of Hole.

Love's proud of the band's early work, especially its first LP, *Pretty on the the Inside,* co-produced by Sonic Youth's Kim Gordon, a hero of Love's, and Gumball's Don Fleming. Still, she says, "That record was me posing in a lot of ways. It was the truth, but it was also me catching up with all my hip peers who'd gone all indie on me, and who made fun of me for liking R.E.M. and the Smiths. I'd done the whole punk thing, sleeping on floors in piss and beer, and waking up with the guy with the fucking mohawk and the skateboards and the speed and the whole goddamned

thing. But I hated it. I'd outgrown it by the time I was 17."
She pauses, grabs a glass of fizzy water, and takes a huge
gulp. "But fuck people if they didn't guess it the first time
around, " she continues, eyes blurring with anger. "If they
didn't get the lucidity. If it's one thing I am, it's lucid. I know
that's not a very heavy word like intellectual or whatever,
but still, to take away my lucidity, that pisses me off."

Live Through This is both a scruffier and more commercial record than Pretty on the Inside. The angsty rants
of yore remain, but they're decorated with a lot more poetry. Milk (as in mother's) is a recurring motif, as is dismem-
berment. Female victimization remains the overall theme,
this time depersonalized into odd, accusatory mini-narra-
tives in which a variety of female characters receive the
protection of Love's tense, manic-depressive singing. Hers
is a natural songwriting talent, full of excellent instincts
and yet wildly unsophisticated. All of which makes Love, in
some ways, a more intriguing figure than, say, Polly
Harvey, Tanya Donelly or Liz Phair, each of whom, idiosyn-
crasies aside, is a traditional talent with an inordinate
knack for the pop tune. It's not inconceivable that Love
might have ended up some kind of peroxided Joni Mitchell
if it weren't for the musical gifts of the diligent, like-minded
Erlandson, and her unstoppable need to fuck with rock
music's male-heavy history.

"Like I was talking to Sophie..." It's a few minutes later,
and Love's relaxing again. "Sophie's done a bunch of
Björk's videos. And Björk is seen as the Icelandic elf child-
woman. But Björk wants to be seen as more erotic. And
I'm like, 'Why?' Elf child-woman is a good job. And my job
as rock's bad girl is good, too. I should just stop trying to
correct people's impressions."

I understand, I say, but it's strange that you're written
off as one-dimensional and didactic when your lyrics, if
anything, tend to err on the side of the abstract.

"That's because I'm not intelligent enough to write
direct narratives," she says sarcastically. "I've always

worked really hard on my lyrics, even when my playing was for shit. So it's weird that when I try to work in different styles, to juxtapose ideas in a careful way that isn't pompous and Byronic, it's just taken as vulgar. The whole cliché of women being cathartic really pisses me off. You know, 'Oh, this is therapy for me. I'd die if I didn't write this.' Eddie Vedder says shit like that. Fuck you."

Misogyny's been a big shock to Love. After all, her parents were '60s quasi-liberals bent on showing their daughter life's brightest profile. The first record she owned was *Free to Be You and Me.* There was a copy of *Our Bodies, Our Selves* sitting on the family toilet for years. She grew up thinking books and records like these were the culture's official textbooks. And she remains an avid reader of feminist theorists like Susan Faludi, Judith Butler, Camille Paglia and Naomi Wolf, though her face crinkles up at the mention of the latter's newest book. "Ugh. Wimp," she crows.

I mention a riot grrrl show she'd helped organize in London last year. Rumor had it the show was a critical and financial disaster, despite the participation of name acts like Huggy Bear, Bratmobile, and Hole. Since that fiasco, the riot grrrl phenomenon has been treated a lot less reverentially in the British music papers. "Yeah, it didn't work," she says, echoing the opinion of other Hole members, male and female. "But then the whole riot grrrl thing is so...well, for one thing, the Women's Studies program at Evergreen State College, Olympia, where a lot of these bands come from, is notorious for being one of the worst programs in the country. It's man-hating, and it doesn't produce very intelligent people in that field. So you've got these girls starting bands, saying, "Well, they printed our picture in the *Melody Maker,* why aren't we getting any royalties?"

"I tried to start a riot grrrl chapter in L.A. at one point. I called a bunch of people to try to set up a meeting, and they were like, 'But the place will be bugged! *A Current*

Affair will be there!' And I'm like, 'Listen, nobody cares, girls. Interest is on the wane in this little fad.'"

No surprise then that Hole's tentative spring tour couples the band not with a "look-alike" band like L7 or Bikini Kill, but with those great bicoastal idiosyncrats Pavement. Love likes them a lot, in part because they're fellow unrepentant Echo and the Bunnymen fans. Still, I sense that there's more than aesthetic compatibility to the pairing. "Remember when Madonna was making the rounds of the clubs scouting bands for her label?" she asks. "Sniffing around people like us and Cell and whoever? Well, a friend and I decided back then that the only cool thing Madonna could do at this point in her career would be to go out with Steve Malkmus." Her eyes get uncharacteristically dreamy. "He's great. It's the Stockton part of him, you know? If it was just the East Coast thing he'd be gross. And he's so well-bred. He's like the Grace Kelly of indie rock."

Our story ends where it began, at 3 PM that same day. Jim Merlis, the genial publicist whom Geffen has assigned to the Hole beat, has just deposited me at the apartment of bassist Pfaff, and is on his way to pick up Love, who doesn't drive. Pfaff's place is stuffed with records, all neatly if unartfully organized along the walls, and there are posters everywhere of her former band Janitor Joe, as well as a few of her favorite band, the Cows.

Eric Erlandson does most of the talking, since Pfaff and Schemel are newcomers. He, like Love, is still reeling from the recent encounter with the drunken journalist. When I turn down a beer, the band's relief is tenable. They seem a pretty sober bunch, if speculation is allowed based on relatively skimpy knowledge. Not to say they spout 12-step rhetoric or anything. But I wait and wait for the drug stories, and when they finally do enter the conversation, it's in a manner so casual and yawny I barely take notice. "Oh, I was so fucked up that night," one of them will say with a bemused wag of the head. Or, "[unnameable celebrity] is such a mess." Later, Love will surprise me even more. Discussing a fellow alternative rock star and Seattle resident's severe heroin problem, she'll chastise the local needle exchange program's home delivery policy, which she thinks only contributes to the severity of the poor guy's habit.

In Lynn Hirschberg's *Vanity Fair* piece, the hard evidence on Love the junked-out monster came via worried quotes from anonymous "friends" and "associates." Having talked to some equally anonymous, long-term friends of hers, what I surmised was that, yeah, like a few of us, she's done some serious drugging in her 28 years. She's been out of control, fucked-up, a complete and utter asshole. She herself refers to periods when "chemicals," as she puts it, were both her major pleasure and obstacle. These mentions may be glancing, but their tone is rich with horror. Partway through the marathon photo shoot, Love spotted Pfaff spacing out on a couch, and rushed over, asking her in this frightened, accusatory voice, "Are you high?!" (She wasn't.) At another point, when I told Love how amused I'd been watching her and Kim Gordon humiliate Dave Kendall on an old episode of *120 Minutes,* she shook her head and said, in this sad, self-incriminating way, "Oh, I was so out of it," then looked grimly off into space.

Maybe the problem is contextual. In *Vanity Fair*'s world, there are two ways to attain power: by leading a glamorous, amoral lifestyle, or by becoming an embittered, subservient, morally superior chronicler of this kind of life. To the latter, Courtney Love is no different than the Barbara Huttons, Demi Moores, and other eccentrics and beauties for whom the bourgeoisie spill their collective saliva. Naively, mistakenly, Love threw her and Kurt Cobain's rough-hewn but essentially moral lives on the mercy of that amoral court because she thought it would be cool. And it was, for those of us who joked about it and rolled our eyes at the subsequent hubbub. If, for one moment, Love thought she could subvert *VF*'s intentions and prove to the world that she wasn't the grunge Valerie Bertinelli or Bianca Jagger, big deal. Nice try. The real question isn't why Love got savaged in the process, or what drugs she did, but rather why we care in the first place.

Is it just that we're starry-eyed misogynists? Twenty or so years ago, our alternative-rock-fan foreparents blamed Yoko Ono and Linda Eastman for the breakup of the very obviously tired and burned-out Beatles. Before meeting the aging moptops, Ono had been a serious Fluxus artist, and Eastman had been an active photojournalist. Back in the '70s, people shredded these two women in print and conversation with the same lazy cattiness we now use to crucify Love, and with even less reason: Nirvana is intact, Cobain is still writing cool shit, Hole is making better and better music, Frances Bean is healthy. The amount of energy expended trying to track and clarify Love's personal quirks is bizarre. Is she really that important?

Me, I like her a lot. And I keep thinking you would too, but then I don't know. Others might tell you different, but I get the impression that, assuming even half of what's been written about Love is true, she's changed. "Changed?" she asks, blinking at my suggestion. She regards me suspiciously for a moment, then squints off into the distance, wondering. "Well, I'm jaded. I've faced every situation for many years with a certain naivete and innocence. But I've somehow become a cynic. Cynicism is a good thing to have on the outside, but it's a terrible thing to have on the inside. All I ever wanted, ever, was to make rock music. Whether it was in the back of a Camaro smoking pot and listening to Journey with some guy who was trying to make out with me, or whether it was the first time I heard the Pretenders. Fuck, Chrissie Hynde really saved me, you know, because she manifested it. She was a pragmatist. Pragmatism is what makes a good songwriter. Pragmatism or drugs. And drug-influenced songs are great, I agree. But I write songs that are clean. Songs that come from here." Love slugs her heart.

Shotgun: The Painting of William Burroughs

Buying into the mythology of William Burroughs at this late stage of its development is hardly the joyously anarchic experience it must have been in 1968. Back then he was the only American novelist capable of decoding contra-cultural fodder like the languages of pornography or technological warfare. Twenty years later, Burroughs is less a literary threat than a celebrity of a very traditional if highly contemporary sort. Think of David Byrne, Philip Glass and Laurie Anderson, just to mention some musicians. Like them he's an oddball vaudevillian whose work does little more than qualify him to hold the attention of certain functional aesthetes. While this may be a less boring spectacle in Burroughs' case (after all he *is* a great writer and moral innovator, etc., who deserves the attention and so on), it's also a lot less engaging, possibly because he seems not to be fully in charge of this stardom's mechanisms the way his younger compatriots are. Certainly the Burroughs persona is a pretty creaky vehicle whose troubleshooting message, constructed of buzzwords for violence and sex, doesn't quite jibe with the courtliness of his presentation.

In the late sixties, Burroughs fired out books in irregular bursts, many of them cannibalizing their predecessors, slaughtering rules as they went along, creating a semi-narrative form that continues to distort not only the way novels are structured and toned (witness Kathy Acker, J.G. Ballard, Clive Barker, William Gibson) but the way songs are recorded (Cabaret Voltaire, The Jesus and Mary Chain, Psychic TV, and Butthole Surfers are among dozens of prominent rock bands who name-check the writer), and even the way the print media organize their information (*Vague, RE/SEARCH, Forced Entries* and *File* have transferred Burroughsian techniques to the idea of the magazine). That's why his adherence to the dated fictional-construct idea of 'the trilogy' for his latest novels (*Cities of the Red Night, The Place of Dead Road* and *The Western Lands*) and, to a lesser extent, their more stated narrative devices, can't help but disappoint, especially since this apparent failure of nerve perpetuates a rather nauseating pattern of revolutionary-type artists accepting the immobility of tradition late in their lives. An obvious example, and the one that bugged me the most as a teenager, was Rimbaud's indoctrination into religious belief on his deathbed.

Burroughs' betrayal of his earlier premise is more banally explicable. As with most of his recent career moves, it seems polished up by a committee of advisers and editors. Older novelists tend to one of two things. Either they write briefer and more concentrated books, as in the case of Samuel Beckett, Italo Calvino, Robert Pinget and others; or they try to collect the ideas of a lifetime into one massive, definite work like Truman Capote, Thomas Pynchon and Harold Brodkey. Burroughs' trilogy would fall into the latter category if only the novels themselves didn't form such a lackadaisical group. Much has been made by reviewers of his new clarity; stories actually begin and end, characters behave consistently. But three clearish narrative fictions in a row do not make a trilogy, no matter how insistent their dust jacket copy. Surely the way to get Burroughs his due is not to package his work so it vaguely resembles what critics tend to respond to, then parade him through the nightclubs of the world with his jaw flapping like a kooky, peripheral character in a TV sitcom.

In director Howard Brookner's excellent biographical film *Burroughs* (1984), the writer was framed from a position within his circle of friends and hangers-on. Soundtracked by the tempestuous drone of his voice reciting various of his works, Burroughs reenacted the characteristics of his myth in docu-drama style, while associates like Allen Ginsberg, Gregory Corso and Terry Southern decorated the clichés (junkie, misogynist, bad father, homosexual) with friendly anecdotes. Brookner's film chronicled and sealed the transformation of Burroughs from the remote scientist of language to the ultra-alternative comedian, of whom the famous Norman Mailer blurb '...the only living American novelist conceivably possessed by genius...' has become a complete anachronism. William Burroughs, stand-up comic, unlike WSB the writer, is only as 'hot' as his latest appearance or two. So it's instructive to study his latest 'routine', a very determined foray into the area of painting, in that ahistorical light but within the context in which it (inadvertently?) competes, the art world circa winter '87-'88.

At a glance Burroughs' paintings looked like the rest of what's going on, meaning they utilized abstract forms with a twist, the twist in this case being rural materials like plywood, crushed and rusted spray paint cans, newspaper clippings and snapshots (including a couple of Burroughs and/or his secretary James Grauerholz). That his first one-person show took place in New York's Tony Shafrazi Gallery, known for its stable of graffiti-related artists like Keith Haring, Kenny Scharf and Ronnie Cutrone, seemed to identify Burroughs as the Grandma Moses of the new geometric art. Actually the comparison isn't as cheap as it sounds, because the Burroughs-as-hip-artist enterprise, as always with an unspecified degree of guidance from Grauerholz, felt indeed like the crudely cynical counterpart to, say, Jeff Koons' sophisticatedly cynical resale of consumer goods to an audience of collectors. The exhibition even managed to simulate an Event, complete with the kinds of mainstream hype the art world hadn't been able to kick up since the early '80s heyday of the neo-expressionist vogue.

The show's scenario, as stated explicitly in the gallery's press release (written by the curator Diego Cortez and available to all visitors), was meant to sound illicit the way Andrew Wyeth's *Helga* paintings were meant to sound illicit without actually revealing anything particularly outré. I quote: 'Indulging in one of his old pastimes—handguns and shotguns—[Burroughs] began target shooting, until one day he picked up the plywood target and noticed how beautiful the object had become with its layers of wood torn away, and he immediately titled it *Sore Shoulder*'. So began a 'five year production of shotgun works,' twenty-four of which were included in this show, along with some related collages and paintings. As for this 'new career for the writer-artist,' Burroughs supposedly hadn't felt comfortable painting because his friend Brion Gysin, painter and inventor of the cut-up method, was a very harsh critic and might have been tough on his fledgling efforts. But now that Gysin was dead, Burroughs, 'perhaps imbued with the spirit of Brion,' felt free to unleash decades of pent-up painterly urges. (This doesn't explain, of course, how Burroughs was able to make the thirteen paintings dated pre-1986, the year Gysin died. Maybe it wasn't that Burroughs couldn't paint with his friend around, just that he couldn't exhibit these slight derivations from Gysin's own underrated if specialized op-styled works.)

The creepiest aspect of this event, aside from the show's naked calculation—whose heavy curatorial defense of Burroughs' talent contradicted our image of a gun-toting visionary—was the clumsy play on viewers' emotions. Cortez referred to the shotgun paintings as 'controversial,' implying a degree of public debate that couldn't have existed, since almost no one had yet seen the paintings. This implication sneakily formed a connection between Burroughs' infamous accidental (and fatal) shooting of his wife during a game of William Tell in the fifties and these 'shotgun' paintings, without seeming to exploit the tragedy. Still, Cortez or somebody did exploit it, as daintily as could be. If 'Burroughs' heart is in this new work,' as the press release stated, and most of the work consisted of 'controversial' bullet holes in plywood targets with blood-like splashes of paint, then didn't these gory, sentimental compositions logically insinuate Burroughs' response to the incident? Somebody hoped so.

In a pamphlet accompanying the exhibition, however, the writer-artist explained the paintings entirely differently. 'To view these pictures puts the viewer in the position of the creative observer,' he wrote, 'who creates by observing.' He then rattled off some of the things he saw in the pictures. 'Here is a Blue Hairy, a creature composed entirely of hair...here is a man pissing against a wall. Behind the wall is a slag heap...Today, Sept. 1, 1987, an animal like a blue ferret with squinty eyes puts it head out of the picture.' He concluded: 'These paintings introduce a new way of seeing. They are not designed to be put on the wall. They are designed to be turned this way and that.' Well, if so, no one bothered to inform Shafrazi, since the paintings were mounted, as immobile as could be, around the walls of the gallery. To have followed Burroughs' instructions and revolved them would have meant having to buy them; I for one couldn't afford it. This show was a mess. The only things remotely controversial about it was how such an incoherent aesthetic premise ever managed to materialize on the walls of a reputable if currently unfashionable gallery.

The general reaction in New York to this show has been ambivalent and full of excuses for the writer, of the order of: he's old, he did his great work, let him dabble. Fine, except that Burroughs is no visual art novice. In fact he has been keeping scrapbooks of cut-up photographs, texts and found images for decades, sometimes as a way to formulate novels, sometimes as a separate and almost diaristic project. Almost none of these works has been exhibited or published. Most are in the Williams S.

Burroughs Archive in Switzerland, although a handful have wound up in the hands of collectors. The three that I saw at a collector's house in 1981 confirmed for me the opinion of some of Burroughs' admirers that they may be his most daring and important work. A better show of the writer's art would have started there, not with these drizzly but more saleable souvenirs of his dotage.

Too Cool for School

It's a breezy, lukewarm Friday evening on a nondescript stretch of East Melrose. Brent Petersen, a graduate student in UCLA's Fine Arts program, is inaugurating his tiny storefront gallery with an exhibit by one of his classmates. A crowd of fellow artists-in-training and faculty members are doing what people usually do at openings: chatting nervously about anything but the art. They're a noisy, dressed-down, twenty-something-heavy crowd. Rumor has it that Petersen, a cherubic if slightly deranged 25-year-old whose artwork involves stalking the Ronald McDonald clown with a video camera, might be playing jokey tribute to the Heaven's Gate mass suicide of the past week by serving Ecstasy-laced applesauce and vodka at the opening. That could explain the healthy turnout.

For most of these students, this is their last year of grad school. In less than two months, they'll do a final group exhibition in one of UCLA's on-campus museums, the faculty will grade them on the fruit of their schooling, and worst-case scenario, they'll be on the street, fast-tracking for day jobs, dropping their slides off at local galleries, and repaying student loans. If that isn't stressful enough, UCLA just happens to be the hottest art school in the country. The art world is watching their every move, and right now could be their one chance to make it. Put another way, if UCLA were a rock scene, it would be Seattle right after *Nevermind* went platinum.

Evan Holloway, 28, and the cause célèbre this evening, is inside one of his artworks, an immense plywood box that takes up most of the gallery. The box houses a soundproofed room just large enough to hold a drum kit, a couple of Evian bottles, and a ventilation tube. Inside,

Holloway plays a loose, amateurish drum solo for as long as he can stand it, which causes the box to emit a faint, muffled rhythm. Like most of the work being created by UCLA students, it's a strange and trippy thing, a kind of special effect masquerading as an art object that appears to be haunted. Or, as someone in the crowd puts it, "This is giving me an acid flashback. And I've never taken acid."

A handful of teenage boys, maybe curious neighbor-hood intruders, just tried unsuccessfully to snag them-selves beers (Petersen opted for a keg rather than the vodka/Ex potion) and have resorted to pressing their ears to the box.

"I think it's playing...what's that Tad song, their MTV hit?" says a floppy-haired kid in a Soundgarden T-shirt.

"Natural One," says his ravey-looking chum.

"No, *Tad*," the boy repeats.

"It's playing 'Natural One,' listen," the second boy insists. "Duh-duh-sh-sh-duh-duh-sh-sh..."

Three of Holloway's school friends, sculptor Tim Rogeberg and painters/musicians Casey Cook and Francesca Gabbiani, have been studying this little scene with knowing grins.

"I like things that when you try to figure them out, your mind snaps," Rogeberg says. He's an affable 25-year-old from Virginia who just this week got snagged by a big local gallery. "I think that's what Evan and lot of us are doing, try-ing to make things that are ungraspable. You can't see the content, you can't see the form. You only see the flip-flop."

"I think it must be hard for people who aren't our age to get our work," adds Cook, 26, a mildly punked-out young blond with a cool if slightly frazzled demeanor. The most successful of the students, she just had her first New York show this past spring. "It comes from our world. You know, the music we listen to, the clubs, the things we talk about."

All of a sudden, the box goes silent. The teenage boys

scrunch up their faces. Holloway's friends get a slightly panicked look. Then a secret door in the box's side pops open and the artist crawls out, dressed in a sweat-soaked gold thrift-store suit. It's not the kind of moment you're supposed to applaud, but Holloway does get a few laconic back slaps as he stumbles towards the gallery's entrance and fresh air.

Artist Charles Ray, a faculty member and one of Holloway's biggest supporters, stops him long enough for a compliment, and wonders aloud if the box will be a part of his final review show.

"Sort of," Holloway says. "I'm going to make a 45. The A side will be the sound of the drums outside the box, and the B side will be the sound of the drums inside the box. And the picture sleeve will have a photo of the exterior of the box on one side, and the interior of the box on the other."

Ray, who claims never to have listened to music, popular or otherwise, when he was growing up, and only figured out when the term rock music meant a year ago when a student made him a Jesus Lizard tape, looks perplexed.

"Trust me," Holloway says, too exhausted to deconstruct the whole indie-rock aesthetic at the moment. "It'll be cool."

The Warner Building is a former factory located in a light industrial area of Culver City, ten miles south of the UCLA campus. The university bought the property in the mid-'80s, and had its interior converted into a maze of studio spaces for graduate students. It looks something like an indoor swap meet crossed with a Halloween spook house; you can get seriously lost in here. Students tell stories of friends, a little stoned or drunk, wandering into the building and getting so confused by the intricate, illogical layout, and so flipped out by the bizarre spread of art, that they're found cowering in the bathroom. Lately, thanks to the buzz around UCLA, the place is swarming with gallery dealers, curators, and collectors from as far away as Europe.

On a basic level, UCLA's success is rather simple to explain: Its teaching staff is a veritable supergroup of well-known artists who, to quote the art critic Peter Schjeldahl, "aim to hit the wrong note squarely." Plus, thanks to UCLA's shockingly low tuition, its students are a blur of social backgrounds, rather than the rich-white-kid hordes that populate most other art schools. And while faculty-student interactions are precious and few, the teachers' clout lets them bring art-world honchos right into their favorite kids' studios. It's just a happy accident that the result is probably the world's top artist-producing machine.

The biggest indicator of UCLA's newfound status may have been this spring's Whitney Biennial, the vast exhibition of sculpture, painting, photography, video and film held every two years at New York's Whitney Museum of American Art. Always controversial, it's also the most important single gig in any young artist's life. the 1997 edition—dubbed "the UCLA Biennial," by art critic Christopher Knight—exhibited a remarkable number of artists associated with the school, either as graduates or teachers. "The art coming out of UCLA is very individualistic," says Lisa Phillips, one of the show's chief curators. "It's refreshingly free of dogma and academic approach. Let's face it, it's hard to make iconoclasm an academy." She doesn't see the work as something entirely new, but rather "something very peculiar. It's amazing how strange the work is to the New York audience in particular." At the same time, "so many people who aren't in the art world have told me that this Biennial has been easier to enter," she says. "It's a very interesting moment."

It's worth pointing out that while a number of UCLA students could soon hit art stardom, it's still nothing like being a rock star. Consider Matthew Barney, arguably the most famous younger artist of the '90s. Ever heard of him? Probably not. The art world is a very small, rarefied place, so invisible to the average person's eye that it's practically a fifth dimension. Occasionally an artist might sneak into popular culture, like Mike Kelley, whose work popped up on the cover of Sonic Youth's *Dirty*. But more often, only an insider could understand the art that's shown in galleries, much less love it. The UCLA crowd hopes to change that. "We don't get our ideas from other art, and that makes a difference," explains Rogenberg. "I think we sense that all that codified, secret-society art you see in most galleries is over."

This afternoon, Liz Craft, a sculpture student, is in the Warner Building's lumber-strewn lobby saying goodbye to a local art dealer named Richard Telles, who recently lured her into his stable of what he calls "younger, experimental, hands-on artists." She has a weird look on her face, which I just assume is the usual pre-career pressures.

"No, I just found out this morning that I live next door to a cop," she tells me. "He's always been really suspicious and weird, but I never imagined he was *that* weird. It kind of puts a new spin on my home life."

Raised in the tiny town of Mammoth Lakes, a ski resort situated on the side of a semi-active volcano in the eastern Sierra Nevadas, Craft is a shy, spacey 27-year-old with huge, anxious eyes. Initially, she enrolled in the undergraduate program of another local university, Otis, majoring in fashion design. "When I was a kid I made weird outfits for myself," she says, leading me through the Warner maze. "So I just figured I'd be a designer. But when I got to school, I realized how crass fashion was." At the encouragement of her painter boyfriend, she switched majors to fine art, and "took a lot of mushrooms, which helped me unlearn a few things." She arrived at UCLA two years ago, and has pretty much been wowing everyone here since.

We sidle past two students fighting over a chain saw,

then squeeze through a pack of young curators from the Museum of Contemporary Art. We happen by Francesca Gabbiani's studio, and I can see her inside, anxiously describing her mystical abstract paintings to two Italian collectors. There's Casey Cook boxing up a painting for her show in New York. A little further along, instructor/artist Paul McCarthy is having Gregg Einhorn demonstrate his latest sculpture to a New York dealer. The piece is a hand-made Colonial dollhouse suspended from the ceiling by invisible wires. The dealer slips his head inside the doll-house and watches an extremely disorienting nature video through the back windows. "Yeah, it's sort of David Lynchian," I hear Einhorn say as we pass.

"It can turn into such a soap opera here," Craft mumbles. "All these people are always here looking around, and we all get so sick of each other. I just hide out in my little world."

Craft unlatches the door of her studio and leads me inside. Her boom box is blasting the Orb, which turns the hammering, drilling, and yelling outside into a faint, tolerable crackle. Most of her studio is taken up by the sculpture she's been working on for the last six months. Part of Craft's brilliance is that her work is so visually discombob-ulating that it reduces commentary to a stammer. All I can say is it looks sort of like a cross between a giant Rubik's Cube and an IKEA display.

"God, I don't know what to say about this," Craft says, blinking at the piece. "You know how at raves there are so many things going on at once? The music's superprimal, but the visuals are so future. You get lost in all that trippy, fun space, all the levels and layers. I'm sort of going for that, I guess. But that sounds so lame."

She flops down on a folding chair, swigs from an Evian bottle, and gives her piece a sad, defeated look. While everyone at UCLA thinks Craft is an unstoppable genius, she's easily as uncertain as any student here, if not more so, especially when it comes to career stuff. Truth is, she finds almost everything outside her art to be kind of bewildering.

"The whole gallery thing kind of sucks," she says. "It's so private, and everything gets treated like it's the Crown Jewels or something. I think my parents could understand my art, and get something out of it, but they'd never go to a gallery in a billion years. I don't even go to them very much. Honestly I think the art world is gross-looking."

Charles Ray—Charley to the students—is in the back-yard of his small West Los Angeles home, working on his newest piece. It's a full-scale fiberglass replica of a severely totalled '91 Pontiac Grand Am, realistic down to the tiniest motor parts, upholstery flaws, and bits of broken windshield. A year ago he bought the original car from police garage. Ray has this idea that the replica will some-how retain the horrific aura of the accident and, at the same time, create the impeccable formal confusion that his work's famous for. It's costing him roughly $120,000 to fabricate. Luckily, he sells everything he makes, so he'll undoubtedly recoup when it's exhibited at an L.A. gallery this fall.

An extremely youthful 44-year-old with the spazzy energy of an adolescent boy and the unpredictable, free-associative speaking patterns of a more together David Helfgott, Ray takes his teaching duties way beyond the classroom. He invites students out on his sailboat, lets them hang out at his studio while he's working, and orga-nizes spontaneous field trips to such unmuseum-like places as the Nixon Library, funny-car shows, and amuse-ment parks, all to get them to think about art's relationship to the non-art-world world. What he's not too crazy about is the media's need to put a label on art, whether it's his or his students'. In other words, he's not at all that wild about me at the moment.

"For a long time, UCLA was like an ivory tower school, very out of touch," he says, kicking one tire after another. "I got here in 1981. Chris Burden [the infamous sculptor and self-destructive performance artist] was already here at the same time, and we were big exceptions to what was a very retro, old-guard group. Around '87, a group of us kind of took over. We dechaired the Chair, pushed out the old farts, and started to fill the department with working artists. Then the school got a lot better."

So what exactly is UCLA's secret?

"None," he says. "Most art schools are about teachers and students. UCLA is about artists working as artists. And UCLA isn't conceptually oriented. You don't have to write a 50-page thesis. You just have to make things. The reason the kids here are getting all this early success is because they're not art students, they're young artists. Young artists get galleries. Students study. Simple as that."

A phone rings in the house. When it stops after two rings, Ray guesses that his girlfriend, artist and UCLA alumna Jennifer Pastor, is home. The kitchen door opens, and Pastor comes out toting their portable phone. She's a sweet-faced, compact 30-year-old. "It's Liz," she says.

Ray grabs the phone. "Yeah, Liz...Have you looked in the gallery where your piece is going to go?...Yeah?... What's nice about that stuff is that it's like the inside of a jellyfish, because it has a linear structure to it....Yeah, just light the trash bag on fire in the kitchen, and say you smelled smoke, because the cops will take ten minutes to get there....No, there's this two-part primer that'll work perfectly. Here, talk to Jennifer. She knows about it." He hands the phone back to her.

"Liz?" Pastor says. "What are you trying to paint?"

Ray heads into the kitchen, tears a banana from its bunch, and puts some water on for coffee. He peels the banana, and shuffles back and forth in the room in a slouchy moonwalk, casting desperate glances at the stove.

"You know what somebody asked me the other day?" He adopts a pinched, European-esque accent. "He said, 'Is

UCLA art a new kind of art that is hemorrhaging into the art world?' And I told him, 'Art hemorrhages into the art world and dies from lack of blood.' You think I like being in the art world? You think any of us do? No. We're there because we have to be there. If we teach the students anything, it's to not let the art world bleed their work to death."

But does he think they're doing something totally new?

"No," he says, obviously frustrated. "Nobody is. But there's something unfamiliar about it, and that's saying a lot."

I tell him how a number of the students I've talked to say mushrooms and acid have helped them see the world more complexly, and how that complexity shows in their work. Could that somehow be the key to their...?

"Oh, Jesus. Every youth culture is druggy." Ray says, and gives me a look like, Why are you telling me this? "That isn't something...look, all I can say is their work isn't about the psychedelic. That's too easy." He walks over to the stove and watches water boil for a few seconds. "To me, what the students are doing is reenchanting the world."

Evan Holloway and his friend Amy Sarkisian, a 27-year-old sculptor, are doing the Friday evening traffic in his dad's '85 Nissan 200SX. They're on a steam-releasing trip to Universal City Walk, a gargantuan theme park-like outdoor mall in the Hollywood Hills. If anything in the world is the antithesis of fine art, they figure it's this consumer-absorbing monstrosity, and besides, they've heard it has a great "3-D vampire ride or something."

The son of hard-core Christian, working-class parents, Holloway grew up in the Los Angeles suburb of Whittier. He left home young, drifted in and out of several universities, and lived for a time in Tacoma, Washington, basically to be near the then-burgeoning grunge scene. If he hadn't been accepted into UCLA, he planned to go to trade school and become a refrigerator repairman. When he first arrived at school he was making messy, charming junk assemblage sculpture that the faculty found "troubling." But in the last year, he's found his voice, as they say. The teachers are more supportive, and Holloway's studio is a regular stop for the invading art honchos. Things look good, but he's "maxing out" his student loans, and most of his work, like the drum box, is too grand and unwieldy to sell. Still, he's easily UCLA's most improved graduate student this year, and for now, that means a lot.

"When I came to UCLA I had no idea what was going on," he says. "I mean I'd heard about Chris Burden's piece where he had a friend shoot him with a rifle and said it was art, and I thought that was cool. But my friends in Tacoma were just guys in bands, and they were completely bewildered by what I was doing. For me, this is the first time in my life that I've been in the right place at the right time."

Holloway parks and we work our way up to Universal City Walk, which looks like the entire Vegas strip squashed onto a plot of land the size of a small high-school campus. After a while we spot a street performer dressed in Hawaiian drag doing a marionette show based on dead rock stars. Dangling from his fingers is a tiny, loose-limbed Kurt Cobain puppet, complete with face-obscuring bands, painted-on stubble, and a plastic guitar-ette. It proceeds to rock out, stage dive, and knock over a miniature amp.

"Oh my God," Holloway laughs, and they go into hysterics, less about the Kurt marionette than the weird puppeteer, who's doing this kind of freaky, ultra-serious ballet. "Do you think he has a girlfriend?"

"And if so, is she proud of him?" Sarkisian adds.

They make it through the little Jimi Hendrix and Jim Morrison numbers, but when Janis Joplin struts on, they're giggled out. Holloway finds them a vacant bench, and they crash there, studying the shoppers and garish storefronts until they're either dead tired or slightly depressed.

"I already miss the Warner Building," Sarkisian says

under her breath.

"I've got to get off my ass," Holloway mumbles. "Or I guess I should. All I want to do is get loaded, go in my studio, and let things happen. My peers and I are really talented, but realistically, we're not all going to get grabbed."

"Yeah, but sometimes I feel like a lot of people at UCLA think showing is more important than the work," Sarkisian says. "I can't see that. Maybe I'm just naive."

"Paul McCarthy talks a lot about making things happen for yourself," Holloway says. "That's what he did, that's what Charley did. But fuck if I know what to do. At least I've got the band."

A guitarist as well as an artist, Holloway recently formed a group, Ovaltone, with fellow students Francesca Gabbiani and Gregg Einhorn. A softly noisy, song-oriented outfit, they've played a few campus gigs, and are angling for a show at Spaceland, L.A.'s grooviest rock club.

"Did I tell you, Amy?" Holloway says. "Brian McMahan, you know of Slint and the For Carnation, saw that last show we did at Warner, and he's going to put in a good word with Spaceland's booker."

"Cool," Sarkisian grins absentmindedly.

Holloway grins too, but it crumbles. Suddenly he's just one tiny figure in a throng of people looking for something extraordinary to do.

"Even if nothing happens, at least I can repair refrigerators," he says. "That's something I learned while working at Starbucks in Tacoma—when refrigerators go down, the world falls apart."

It's 4 AM, a few days later. The Warner studios are packed with frazzled students working overtime to get their pieces in shape for the final review show, now less than three weeks away. Tim Rogeberg is polishing off his contribution, a mobile-like mini-solar system of planet-esque sculptures that, fingers crossed, will resemble an extremely fucked-up astronomical science demonstration. Having waterproofed his studio's floor, he's about to flood the space with a pool of chemicals when he yells to Holloway in the studio next door. "We need a blow-out or something," he tells me. "Everybody's bickering over tools and things. I'm thinking about throwing a party that's more like a collaboration, kind of a performance piece. Something to get us all working together." Holloway arrives, and he's happy to help. By the time they crash on the couches that litter the building, it's dawn, and there's an announcement chalked out on the Warner blackboard. PARTY HERE TONIGHT, it reads. BLOOD WRESTLING. KEG. MUST WEAR COSTUME.

By ten the next evening, the place is a zoo, maybe 30 students, each one overdressed to freak. Holloway is wearing a gigantic, upside-down Christmas stocking with holes cut out for the face and the arms. It takes everyone a weirdly long time to recognize Craft beneath her afro wig, feather boa, fishnet stockings, and stilettos. Gregg Einhorn has gone the Dada route with a pointed paper hat, oversized beak, and angel's wings. Rogeberg's character is called Trippy Longstocking, which I suppose is self-explanatory. Francesca Gabbiani is a "pregnant '70s chick." And Sarkisian keeps disappearing into her studio to change costumes, from the Unabomber to the Zodiac Killer and back again, because "I think they're the same person."

In the middle of the floor is an inflatable plastic kiddie pool which Rogeberg has filled with a mixture of stage blood, jelly, Kool-Aid, and chocolate. Students have been shoving each other in its direction all night, but no one's taken the plunge. Then someone knocks Holloway into the gory liquid, and a free-for-all erupts. Two messy hours later, it's down to a wrestling match between Craft and Holloway. Most of the students have gone home by now, but a hard-core "blood"-soaked handful remain, cheering hoarsely for their favorite. Craft may wind up the most celebrated artist of her generation, and Holloway may spend his life fixing refrigerators and making weird contraptions in his basement, but tonight they're just interchangeable pieces of a wacky extravaganza that has UCLA stamped all over it. It's no big deal necessarily. Still, it's not quite like anything I've ever seen, and I can understand what Ray meant. I'm entranced. It's hard to say if this is an apt metaphor for the whole UCLA aesthetic, or just a bunch of drunken weirdos having fun the only way they know how. Anyway, if I asked them which, they'd probably just push me into the pool.

Junkie See, Junkie Do

When an Alice in Chains video comes on MTV, most of us either crank the volume, or immediately change channels. But heroin addicts and struggling former addicts hear something in Layne Staley's grade-school junkie poetry that we can't: a kind of siren. As someone who has had several close friends who were strung out on heroin in the past two years, I think I have a sense of how this private call-and-response works, even if I can't understand the mechanisms. According to my friends, just the mention of the word "heroin" in a lyric, or a photograph of a hypodermic on a CD cover, or the sight of junkie musicians all wrapped up in some glamorous video, and they go crazy with longing for the stuff, even when, as in the case of Alice in Chains, they know full well that what they are hearing and seeing is silly and contrived. Recently, I saw one of the most intelligent people I know absolutely freak out watching the old Thompson Twins video "Don't Mess With Doctor Dream." One minute we were guffawing at its cheesy imagery—spinning needles, screaming skulls, sanctimonious antidrug captions— and the next minute he was a jittery wreck begging me to drive him downtown so he could buy a few bags.

Can I blame MTV? Maybe, at least according to Michigan's Institute for Social Research (ISR). It recently conducted a survey in which 50,000 high school students around the U.S. were asked about drugs. According to the study, drug use is on the rise again. Big surprise. And Dr. Lloyd D. Johnston, program director of ISR, thinks the problem lies in the representation of drug use in contemporary music, films, and rock videos. Like generations of academics before him, he sees teenagers as a kind of intellectually passive, easily seduced herd in need of strict parental guidance. Never mind that this conclusion is pure speculation, and not based on data actually unearthed by the survey. In this confused world of ours, even the appearance of fact attains a kind of godlike status, and statisticians, those great cultural simplifiers, are considered something on the order of gods. Thus, when the *New York Times* reported the results of this survey, Johnston's ruminations were treated as though they were the story, and the teens' statements were lost in the shuffle. It's all spurious, but coming on the heels of the aforementioned Thompson Twins fiasco it got me to wondering whether Johnston has a point.

Donna Gaines, sociologist and author of *Teenage Wasteland: Suburbia's Dead End Kids,* doesn't think so. She sees youth culture and drug use as historically enmeshed. "With MTV, drug use has just taken on the status of a commodity," she says. "When I was younger and some actress was wearing a really cool miniskirt in a movie, I wanted that miniskirt. Now when you see some guy getting fucked up on MTV, you want to get fucked up. But videos are expressive rather than coercive. I don't see it as a causal relationship. Anyway, most hard-core drug users don't watch MTV. Its audience is mainstream. And I don't think it's such a great cultural force anyway. Maybe for 12-year-olds."

Video director Samuel Bayer, who has worked with Nirvana and Hole among others, gives MTV more credit, but thinks the network is sufficiently prudent in its policies. "I grew up in the '70s, when there were drug references all over the place," he says. "Kids are smart enough to read between the lines. Something like Kurt Cobain dying—that's what happens when your life is fucked up. If anything, videos have the opposite effect."

In the same *New York Times* article that reported Johnston's findings, Carole Robinson, a senior vice president at MTV, said that the network's guidelines call for programming that does not "promote, glamorize, or show as socially acceptable the use of illegal drugs or the abuse of legal drugs." And anyone who watches MTV regularly has noticed those little Tinkerbell-like digital blurs clinging to the pot leaves on hip-hop artists' caps. In the current Tom Petty video, a line about rolling a joint has been auditorially altered into a nonsensical slur. Especially since Cobain's death, the network's non-music programming has been nearly didactic in its cautionary tone regarding hard drug use. Still, you don't need a degree in deconstruction to see the signs of drugginess all over MTV, whether it's Alice in Chains' elegant little travelogues of junkie life, or Ministry's "Just One Fix" clip, in which heroin withdrawal is given a snazzy, action-packed movie-trailer look, or even Tori Amos's clip for "God," in which a character simulates "tying off." If kids are smart enough to know what's fiction and what's not, then they are smart enough to decode these kinds of messages too.

If MTV has a drug policy, it's a confused one. It is as if the network had chosen to approach drug-related videos the way a makeup artist might approach crow's-feet on an aging actress. Pot leaves, pills, and hypodermic needles are successfully smudged beyond recognition, but the subtleties remain. Maybe this kind of approach works with drugs such as pot, cocaine, and acid, although I doubt it. But heroin is a complicated beast with a very subtle system of signifiers, most of which are invisible to nonusers' eyes. Take the aforementioned Ministry clip. To MTV, it must read as an anti-heroin statement, with a surface narrative in which two young junkies detox in a shabby hotel room intercut with shots of heroin icon William S. Burroughs waving his hands in a cautionary manner a la the giant alien in *Twin Peaks*. But look closer and there's old Al Jourgensen himself slouched in the hotel's lobby. In one telling close-up, he looks at the camera and rubs his nose with one finger. It's a nervous tic common to junkies, and a signal to knowledgeable viewers that Jourgensen, or rather his character, is loaded on the stuff. So later when the boys leave the hotel, supposedly detoxed and ready for the world, and Jourgensen picks them up hitchhiking, there's a definite subtext, i.e., they'll be shooting up again any minute.

A few weeks ago, I happened to catch Primal Scream's "Rocks" video on MTV's "Alternative Nation." Primal Scream is a U.K. band whose work flaunts the meagerness of its members' imagination and technical ability. Its records are affectionate pastiches of other, more talented bands' music, past and present. It's all very postmodern. In its current incarnation, Primal Scream is pretending to be junkie rock. Keith Richards, Johnny Thunders, and Gram Parsons are the obvious models. Last year, the band even caused a little scandal in the British rock music press by jokily referring to the late River Phoenix as a "lightweight." In the "Rocks" clip, frontman Bobby Gillespie stumbles around slurring about the joys of unmitigated hedonism. His hair is long and filthy, his skin has the hue of a corpse, and his mouth hangs partway open in an imitation of someone nodding out on his feet. I think you're supposed to be bemused. But all I could think about while watching this freak show was what my troubled friend would do when he saw him.

Because heroin withdrawal is such an agonizing process, and the recovery period so long and psychologically disruptive, it doesn't take much to make former addicts slip. Heroin may be a nasty business on a day-to-day basis, but the drug's immediate effect is profoundly pleasurable. My friends say it is like the ultimate orgasm, elongated and unattached to the rest of the world. Its intensity, they tell me, makes life's relatively sober comforts like friendship, romance, and sex seem petty. So reentering the world in which these things are generally held as sacred can feel, I'm told, like a compromise, especially in the first year or so, when your body's gradual reconstruction causes almost continual discomfort. Thus even something like Kurt Cobain's suicide, which most of us interpret as the ultimate anti-heroin statement, has a double meaning. For instance, the morning I heard the news, I phoned up a Nirvana fan I knew who was struggling to stay off dope, and begged her to please fucking quit before she ends up like him. "No," she said, her voice edgy with a hunger and anger I couldn't decode. "You don't understand." And she explained how Cobain's inability to stay clean only reinforced her feeling that sobriety wasn't worth the trouble. When I hung up the phone I knew she was going to run out and score. And she did.

When I was a young teen listening to the Velvet Underground and John Lennon's "Cold Turkey," and reading William S. Burroughs and Alex Trocchi, I never—and I think I can include my former friends in this—thought "Hey, I should try this heroin stuff." Presumably most kids are the same way now. But a number of young rock fans have started shooting heroin because one or more of their heroes has made light of the subject. I know a handful of them myself. I'm talking about talented, smart people who just want to experience everything that there is to experience. To them, River Phoenix convulsing on the sidewalk, or Kristen Pfaff nodding out in a lukewarm bath—these things are as faraway, unreal, and mythical as the song lyrics that render heroin use a profound, sensual voyage into the mysteries of the self. Some people will always choose to do extreme things. Others, maybe most of us, will choose to learn by listening to songs about extreme activities, or by reading nonfictional accounts. So how do those of us who don't really understand what it means to shoot heroin tell users to stop what they're doing because it's scaring us? Well, we can't. But we can air our fears and presumptions and hope for the best.

A former member of several prominent alternative rock bands, who requested anonymity, spoke to me about his own confusion around the representation of heroin in videos. A former junkie, he has been clean for several years. "I can see both sides," he says. "When you're doing dope, it permeates everything you do and think. It feels like enlightenment, and you also feel really alone at the same time, so you want to network. It's not even a conscious thing. I can't even watch MTV anymore, it's so full of junkies. I can spot them in an instant, and I feel like they're calling to me from this terrible and fascinating place in my past. The thing is, they're some of the most interesting musicians around, so it would be crazy to shut them up. So it's just this tortuous paradox." So the only option he sees is looking the other way?

"What other way?" he says. "That's what heroin does, removes you from the scariness in the world. I found out that doesn't work either. If there is an option, it's being strong, and believing in your loved ones. Because every-thing else, including drugs, is just meaningless entertain-ment."

Point is, even if MTV could eliminate every shred of every drug reference in every video, it wouldn't make any difference, and it would only cause the network to seem even more untrustworthy than it already is. Why should MTV be self-censorious when the record, television, and film industries are expected to support artistic freedom of expression? Pop culture is a mishmash of images of every type of behavior and attitude. It presents a chaotic, multi-tudinous portrait of life that becomes a kind of collective truth which we are then responsible for decoding and using according to our own personal needs at any given moment. For every positive portrayal of drug use, you can be sure there's a negative one somewhere else. It's a bal-ance, and that's fine, because, as painful as it may be to watch friends suffer because of some irresponsible rock star's posey bullshit, we have no control over one another's lives. We choose people to love according to psychological systems that are nobody's business but our own. And if we suffer as a consequence of our love, them's the breaks.

The Ballad of Nan Goldin

I inadvertently stumbled into Nan Goldin's world in 1987. Hopelessly in love with a young Dutch playwright, I'd left New York for Amsterdam to be near him and to finish my first novel, which had crapped out thanks to a nasty cocaine habit and a last pre-safe-sex stampede of promiscuity. A year later, my boyfriend and I were enemies. I'd replaced coke with crystal meth, and barely cracked the lid on my laptop.

When I wasn't storming in and out of my boyfriend's apartment, I was hanging out in Amsterdam's slew of boy brothels, doing drugs with the hustlers and copping the occasional freebie. I'd hoped to purify my life with love and isolation-induced hard work. But all I'd done was graft my bad habits into a lonelier, more exotic locale. Like all addicts, I wasn't particularly happy or miserable. I was just sort of there, cornered, one more American expatriate who thought he was Rimbaud, treating chemicals as though they were alchemical, with no will or energy to make my dazed explorations into anything resembling art. One day I read in the newspaper that something called *The Ballad of Sexual Dependency* was being shown at the local art museum, and, intrigued by the title—not to mention titillated by the accompanying illustration of a cute young hipster with a needle in his arm—I stumbled into the theater.

The Ballad of Sexual Dependency is a slide show. Rather, it's a kind of documentary film in the guise of a slide show, incorporating 45 or so minutes of slowly crossfading images of Goldin and her friends through the years, accompanied by a rough medley of sad love songs past and present, from Marlene Dietrich's "Falling in Love Again" to Television's "Venus de Milo." Organized by subject, it depicts with loving attentiveness and absolute amorality the day-to-day lives of smallish gangs of reasonably hip young people—male, female, straight, gay, drag queens, artists, punks—as they party, drink, do drugs, suffer hangovers, fuck, fight, and fall in and out of love. Some of the images are as casual as any snapshot taken at any social gathering. Others are as dramatic and lushly beautiful as noir film stills. Together they tell a story that has no story per se, but is rather an intimate ebb and flow of bodies, especially faces, lost in private drug and/or endorphin-fueled utopias. It's hard to imagine in light of recent films like *Kids* and *Trainspotting* how astonishing it felt to be given such a careful, intimate, unqualified view of so personal a world, but at the time there was nothing like it.

"I remember being in a club, upstairs somewhere, when I first saw *Ballad*," says writer/critic Lynne Tillman, a longtime friend of Goldin's. "A lot of people had been making Super-8 sound films, and Nan's slide show seemed connected to that. But you felt immediately that the concept was different. It was about being exhaustive; including everything she knew. It's like the way she takes notes about everything. She used to do that when we met, wrote things down as we said them." Novelist Linda Yablonsky, a friend of Goldin's since the early 1980s, concurs. "When I saw *Ballad*, the accumulated power of images hurt me, all that beauty and pain, and I cried," she says. "I knew those people, and she really captured it. In most photographs, people don't really look like themselves. In *Ballad*, they looked absolutely like themselves."

As for me, I..."You felt like that was your life up there?" Goldin says, completing my sentence. "Yeah, I hear that a lot." Goldin is in Berlin, putting the finishing touches on the catalog that will accompany "I'll Be Your Mirror," her fall mid-career retrospective at New York's Whitney Museum of American Art. I'm in Los Angeles, finishing my fourth novel. I feel like I owe her something, and I try to tell her so. Somehow, after I saw *Ballad* that day in Amsterdam, I never quite lost myself in drugging and promiscuity with the same intensity or lack of composure again. It was as if, through her pictures of lives so much like mine, my own fucked-up behavior acquired a look, a narrative coherency, an aesthetic. Even now when I think back on some of the shit I pulled, at some of the bottoms I hit, the memories are distinctly Goldin-esque. I can see the rooms where I snorted drugs, fucked hustlers, screamed at my boyfriend; I keep thinking that if I'd had the wherewithal to approach her that day, I might have cleaned up a little sooner. "It's just as well you didn't bother me," she says. "I'm sure all I was thinking about was how I could cop. I was definitely hitting bottom in those days."

Nan Goldin was born on September 12, 1953, in Washington, D.C., and grew up in Silver Spring, Maryland, the youngest of four children in a "defiantly middle-class" family. She was especially close to her older sister Barbara, an intelligent, rebellious girl who played piano brilliantly. When Nan was 11, Barbara killed herself by lying down on some railroad tracks just outside Washington. Devastated, Nan ran away from home several times that year, and was eventually placed in foster care by her parents. "I basically got farmed out to rich people," she says. "But eventually they threw me out because I was growing pot in their greenhouse, and because I had a black boyfriend."

By 1972, she'd found a "new family," seven fellow artsy, androgynous teenagers with whom she shared a railroad apartment in Boston. Her favorite among them was David Armstrong, a skinny, effeminate gay boy just beginning to experiment with drag. He became Goldin's lifelong best friend, most frequent subject, and, as she puts it, "the eye of my storm." Now a respected photographer himself, Armstrong remembers those days as "just a really wonderful time. Nobody had any money. I was occasionally turning tricks. That summer of '72, Nan really started photographing a lot, and our lives revolved around that." "I started taking pictures because of my sister's suicide," Goldin says. "I'd lost her. And I became obsessed with never losing the memory of anyone ever again."

For teenagers who were keyed into rock'n'roll culture of the early '70s, art and life seemed gorgeously indistinguishable. It was a time of glam rock, surely the strangest and headiest subculture to have splintered from late '60s hippiedom. Hippies might have talked stylistic and sexual freedom, but with the exception of period freaks like the Velvet Underground, Andy Warhol, and Iggy Pop, that movement's drift was in fact anti-style, grubby even, and comfortably heterosexist. But by 1973, thanks to the influence of Warhol, director John Waters, and gender-bending rockers like David Bowie and the New York Dolls, gays and other sexual outlaws had a scene of their own, a modus operandi with which to flirt openly if surreptitiously with the youth of America. For Goldin, it was enough to document the goings-on. She harbored dreams of being a fashion photographer, and of putting her drag queen friends on the cover of Vogue. "I just didn't see how I could make it as an artist at that point," she says. The idea of producing little glam souvenirs for New York gallery goers bemused her, but it was out of the question, like wanting to get your parents stoned.

As a result, that era from the dawn of Glam to the incursion of Punk is remembered the way a party is remembered, through random snapshots of besotted, campily dressed, mugging participants. The genius of *The Ballad of Sexual Dependency*, perhaps the deepest visual record of that period, is almost accidental. Goldin snapped her trendy friends out of love and fear, purely to preserve their essence, to prevent them from leaving her without a trace. In one of those lucky, mysterious coincidences that distinguish artists from artistes, Goldin happened to possess an incredible eye for the multidimensionality of her surroundings. Her pictures not only did justice to whatever poses her friends wished to strike, they nailed the sometimes incongruous emotions that inspired the poses. Freed from the issues of commerce that qualify the work of career artists, Goldin could be the girl with the camera, the friend whom everyone instinctively turned to at moments of bliss, sadness, lust, et cetera, knowing they'd get a trustworthy record. If they'd thought their mugs would wind up on gallery walls, maybe they wouldn't have given themselves up so resolutely. But they knew that a few days later they'd be sitting around Goldin's apartment, stoned and guffawing as she clicked off the slides, and the Stooges played on the stereo.

This is not to say that Goldin didn't take her photography seriously even then. In the mid-'70s she enrolled in the School of the Museum of Fine Art in Boston. While she considers the work she did there "the worst I'd ever done," too clouded with bourgeois polish, too sapped of intimacy, she did learn to make color prints and use a wide-angle lens. Also attending the school were some like-minded young artists who were equally cowed by the idea of art-world careers. There was Mark Morrisroe, whose punky, invasive, homoerotic self-portraits are only now being appreciated, ten years after his AIDS-related death. And there was Jack Pierson, later Morrisroe's lover, whom Goldin would meet in New York in 1985. Pierson's fey, melancholic, mock-bland snapshots of modelly hunks would later make him one of the biggest art stars of the early '90s. They, Goldin, and Armstrong would later be seen as a kind of movement, the so-called "Boston School," early and influential progenitors of an artful, aggressive casualness that is currently de rigeur in the art world. But at the time they were just a bunch of druggies and fags who wanted to be artists, and their camaraderie wasn't enough to prevent Goldin, Armstrong, and his lover Bruce Balboni from fleeing to New York and its famous Downtown scene of artsy punk rockers and punky young artists.

When Goldin arrived in 1978, punk had already gobbled up what was left of glam. Androgyny and, to a certain extent, fagginess were still relatively cool, thanks to crossover veterans like the Dolls and Wayne County, but it was really, *really* cool to make a show of displaying your pain, boredom, rage and disaffection. These were exactly the depths that Goldin had always been interested in recording, and people began to pick up on her work. Goldin and her friends became denizens of the legendary Mudd Club, where, as part of a celebration of Frank Zappa's birthday, she gave her first public slide show. By then she had gathered most of the coterie of pals who would make up the cast of *Ballad*—Armstrong, Balboni, writer/underground film star Cookie Mueller, Mueller's love Sharon Niesp, transsexual artist Greer Lankton, and others. Emboldened by her Mudd Club success, Goldin photographed her friends and herself ever more obsessively, and worked on the slide show, adding its soundtrack and eventually giving it a name.

Soon, *The Ballad of Sexual Dependency* began to attract attention both in and outside the art world. Critics compared the work to the early films of Warhol and John Cassavetes. Screenings were events. *Aperture* published a best-selling collection of the slide-show's images. Museums, nightclubs, and alternative art spaces around the world flew Goldin in to present *Ballad*. The high-powered gallery Pace/MacGill added her to its blue-chip roster. But in her life, and in the lives of many of her friends/subjects, the innocent drug play of what Goldin calls "the party years" had escalated into full-scale, horror show-like addiction. Her photographs recorded the downward swing, even if she was too doped up to see the change. Armstrong, whose androgynous, bewitching face dominates Goldin's early images became a sweaty, disheveled junkie sprawled on a couch. "All that glamour that had been attached to getting high," he remembers, "was hard to hold onto. Then there was no glamour left at all." Even Goldin began to avoid her best friend. "I hated to pity him," she says. Vibrant, wacky Lankton grew scrawny and zizzed. Balboni, an early modern-primitive type, started to look like some homeless guy who accidentally wandered into frame. Across the board, people either packed on the pounds or deflated, their kingdoms no longer the latest clubs and cafés but rather the shadowy depths of their messy drug-departments.

Goldin, meanwhile, had fallen in love. The relationship, which she describes as "intense, jealous, sexual, and bonded by drugs," became to the center of her work. In pictures at least, Brian was a fearsome-looking character who seems to have two emotions, sullenness and rage. "No one could understand what she saw in him," says an acquaintance from the period. "They did nothing but fight." "Nan was way out there," adds another friend of this period. "She looked crazy. She got in a lot of fights with people, physical fights, and she alienated a lot of friends. It was very hurtful." At he time, Goldin was too gone to care. "Brian was really gorgeous for a while, and emotionally we fit," she says. "It was kind of like being in a wild three-way—me, my lover, and the drugs. I'd started shooting dope when I was 18, and I'd been able to stop, put it down with no problem. I just thought, 'Nothing can get me,' you know?"

One night in Berlin in 1984, where Goldin had come to show *Ballad*, she and Brian had a particularly nasty blow-out, during which he beat her so badly that she had to be hospitalized. "The guy hit her in the face, in the eyes, which seemed particularly cruel considering she's a photographer," says someone formerly associated with the couple in Berlin. "She was really hurt, and it didn't seem like her friends knew how to deal, probably because of the drugs and all that. She seemed very alone." Goldin shot a series of photographs of her battered face, "so I would never go back to him" Still, her drug addiction worsened, and she began to hole up in her New York loft. Armstrong, who'd gotten clean by that point and was living back in

Boston, accepted her request to move in and take care of her, but things were too squalid and he bailed after one day. Goldin's only self-portrait from this time is a blurry, haphazard-looking shot of her sitting on her bed, talking on the phone, dead-eyed, obese, and surrounded by ashtrays.

"It was pathetic," she says. "All I did was lie in bed and watch *I Love Lucy* reruns. There was no day or night. Nobody would deal with me. I guess that's what did it, the loneliness. But even so, I went into rehab not as a decision to get clean but as a decision to get methadone. But when I got there I was so disoriented I realized that I couldn't go on, and I gave in."

"Nan wrote me a letter when she was in rehab," remembers Yablonsky, who had herself cleaned up after a six-year-long drug addiction. "She said they had taken her camera away, and she didn't know what to do. Her work was her life. She had a hard time separating the two." When she was well enough to go to a halfway house, her camera was returned to her. She began taking simple self-portraits, sitting on her bed, standing by a tree. "It was during this time that I rediscovered daylight," she says. "I needed to relearn my face." By 1990, she felt strong enough to move back to New York. Armstrong accompanied her, and together they tried to reform their extended family, or what was left of it.

Where once Goldin had photographed her friends to keep them alive, to prevent anyone she knew from disappearing, now it was all about savoring the last drops: Cookie Mueller thinning, thinning, glazing over, and finally lying in her coffin. Her German friend Alf, spooky-eyed but otherwise fit, then suddenly bandaged and dead in a hospital bed. Her French art dealer Gilles transforming from a suave, tattooed hunk into a concave, expressionless skeleton. David Armstrong, Bruce Balboni, Sharon Niesp, et al., grimly dealing with it all.

A lot of photographers have explored AIDS and its consequences in their work. There's an undeniable power to all these photos, whatever their maker's skills or purity of intention. You take a picture of someone sick or unhappy, it's going to function, if for no other reason than it triggers compassion. It was Andy Warhol who said, "People are so great, you can't take a bad photograph." But the force of Goldin's work is more than coincidence. She knew her friends when they were beautiful and crazy, and she knew them now when they were fucking her over by dying, proving her to be powerless after all. Somehow, her pictures radiate that knowledge.

Still, too much knowledge can be a dangerous thing. So as a way of shaking off all that death, Goldin returned to square one. In 1991, she started shooting New York's drag queen renaissance, the hyperactive nightlife that had sprouted around clubs like Jackie 60 and Squeezebox, and the Wigstock Festival. "I really hadn't been around the queens for 20 years," she says, "and it had changed so much. Drag had become completely accepted. I saw it as probably the most hopeful, positive part of the gay world at that point."

Around the same time, she began a collaboration with the Japanese photographer Nobuyoshi Araki, documenting Tokyo's youth culture. The results, collectively titled *Tokyo Love*, were published in book form in the United States last year. It's perhaps her sweetest, most tender-hearted body of work. Paradoxically, it's also been her most controversial, causing some critics to claim she had merely simplified and exoticized a foreign culture. "Yeah, the PC police," she says. "No, I was just fascinated by the beauty and wildness of those kids. It was like going back to my adolescence. I saw Japan as this country where there was a simulation of wildness, without drugs, without AIDS, neither of which where much of an issue there. For them, it seemed to be more about style, and the appropriation of style, with no real understanding of what it all means. It seemed like a return to paradise. Those kids weren't self-destructive like my friends and I were."

In a week, Nan Goldin will leave Berlin and return to New York, then spend the next two months dealing with the minutiae around the retrospective. After all that's over, she'd like to think about making a film. She recently co-directed a BBC documentary on her life, also titled *I'll Be Your Mirror*, and found the experience curious. "The thing about film versus the slide show is that in film everything's stuck," she says. For example, she tells me, since the BBC documentary was made, "David has lost 30 pounds and looks gorgeous. Sharon lost 30 pounds and broke up with her girlfriend. Bruce started shooting up again, but he's clean now..." Otherwise, her agenda includes more photographing, probably landscapes and portraits of children and "hopefully more pleasure." The latter has something to do with that fact that, after six years of sobriety, Goldin started drinking again a year and a half ago while in Japan, a decision that concerns some of her sober friends. "I love being sober," she says, "I just wish I could be sober *and* drink. It hasn't been a big crisis for me. It's more a problem for people who are still in the program. When I was sober I was a total workaholic. I had an absolute vision of things, and everything was too compartmentalized. Now I have more tolerance of the variations. It's not all light, and it's not all dark. Not that I have anything against the program at all. It saved my life. I think I just outgrew it."

Like I said, when I saw *The Ballad of Sexual Dependency* back in 1986, I saw eerie parallels between Goldin's chaotic world and my own. From what I can gather, the parallels continue. Like me, and like most of the people that we both know, she seems to have gotten her shit together by becoming an artist first and a fun-seeker second. Not to sound like John Tesh at the Summer Olympics, but I can't help but wonder what, if anything in particular, is on the artist's mind at this, her proverbial moment of triumph. In the art world, a Whitney retrospective is the closest you get to a gold medal.

"Well, I guess I think about my sister," says Goldin,

sounding not unlike an Olympic athlete for a moment. "Her death completely changed my life. I'm constantly looking for the intimacy I had with her, in my life and my work. And I think about the deaths of my friends. My sister's death is more abstract to me, more symbolic. Their deaths are real, and that's left behind this immense legacy. That's why I photograph. I miss so many people so badly."

Sonny Rising

Beverly Hills City Hall is one of those fake period buildings so beloved of middlebrow SoCal architects. Blandly Spanish, vaguely colonial, it exists only to blend in with the decades-older public library nearby. For some reason, it was also chosen as the venue for Congressman Sonny Bono's entertainment-industry summit. Pulled together in the wake of Bob Dole's mega-publicized attacks on rap music and on openly violent and/or sexy films, this fact-gathering session—as it's being billed—provides freshman congressman Bono with a golden opportunity to overcome his public image as the lesser half of Sonny and Cher and establish a coherent role for himself within the Republican Party.

When Bono first arrived on the Hill in 1994, he seemed determined to induce amnesia about his pop-song past, presenting himself more as businessman than entertainer. But Dole's comments have inadvertently given Bono's showbiz credentials a new luster. As for Bono's own feelings about Dole's provocative if rather generalized swipe at the industry he once called home, the congressman has chosen to work the middle ground. While he admits to sharing Dole's outrage at art that crosses the line "not just of taste, but of human dignity and decency," he thinks the senator's approach, which he has characterized as nose-wrinkling, is ill-conceived. The summit meeting seems to be Bono's attempt to do what he calls a little partisan "damage control." His stated goals are twofold—to open lines of communication between the Republicans and Hollywood and to suggest, as tactfully as possible, that the American public is on Dole's side.

In Hollywood, the Democrats are so ingrained in the woodwork they practically are the woodwork. President Clinton pointedly schmoozed with the stars in his '92 campaign, and Hollywood talent often throws its images and money behind Democratic candidates, no matter how minor the campaigns. In contrast, the Republican Party tends to interface with the entertainment industry at the corporate level. Sure, the Mighty Morphin Power Rangers showed up to cheer Newt Gingrich at the opening of the 104th Congress. And an odd array of Hollywood notables, including Kevin Costner, Delta Burke, Shannen Doherty and Chris Farley, have rallied to the Republican cause in public. But such acknowledgments are rare enough to seem freakish.

Way back in the silent-film era, Hollywood was dominated by conservatives. Studio heads such as MGM's Louis B. Mayer produced movies long on the very family values now lionized by Republicans. Stars' opinions reached the public preprocessed by a well-oiled publicity machine, in which everyone worked together to protect the industry's magical image. With the advent of talking pictures, actors from the East Coast theater scene flooded out to Hollywood and brought more liberal values with them. Still, the conservative agenda held preeminence.

McCarthyism and the blacklist changed all that, causing the industry to reevaluate its priorities. Liberalism seemed the only value system that offered the artistic community protection from future assaults on its patriotism. Nowadays, it would seem outrageous to suggest that television and movies should adhere to a single, coherent moral structure, and conservatives within the industry are forced to work in much the same molelike way as did the industry's Communist-sympathizers of an earlier era. "I've heard from many stars who are afraid they'll lose work if they come forward as Republicans," says Jennifer Smith, president of the Smith Fairfield consulting firm, which links Republican celebrities to party fundraisers. "The studios are all owned by Democrats."

The fact is, even now there are Republicans working quietly at every level of the entertainment industry. And while Bono seems determined to flush them out, what he must understand is that Hollywood conservatives are different from the conservatives in the rest of the country at whom Dole aimed his calculatedly emotional appeal. *Pulp Fiction*, a chief object of conservative critique, not only costarred proud Republican Bruce Willis, it made more than $100 million and influenced a slew of other filmmakers. To expect prominent industry Republican supporters such as producer Jerry Weintraub to attack director Quentin Tarantino's aesthetic choices is like expecting Dole to attack Newt Gingrich's syntax.

Therefore, Bono faces a herculean and historic task. He needs to so inspire sympathizers within Hollywood that they will be willing to risk their already tenuous industry power to become missionaries for a vague, unfashionable notion of the common good. This would seem a rather grand role for Bono, an entertainer whose name, for some two decades, has most commonly been heard on the lips of Trivial Pursuit players. He served a few years as mayor of Palm Springs, then ran in 1994 for the congressional seat of California's Forty-fourth District, the so-called Inland Empire—a huge expanse of smoggy semidesert so densely populated with Republicans it makes Orange County seem like San Francisco. It's no surprise that, after hammering home a terse, user-friendly, soft-core conservative agenda to any book club or Rotary Club meeting that would have him, Bono won his seat rather handily.

No question Bono's celebrity was the key factor in winning him the election, but until Dole's anti-Hollywood sound bite, it didn't do him any favors back in Washington. Now with film and television suddenly on the official agenda, Bono has found himself in a new spotlight. And he's working it, to say the least. In early 1995, he lobbied House Speaker Gingrich to allow him to head the House of

Representatives' newly formed Entertainment Task Force. He buddied up to David Horowitz, former editor of the defunct leftist magazine *Ramparts* and now head of the ultraconservative Center for the Study of Popular Culture— a nonprofit organization located in Studio City, with an agenda that includes trying to harass powerful liberals in the entertainment industry into an early retirement. Then Bono hit the talk show circuit, this time with a lot more on his mind than his ex-wife.

In April 1995, Bono chaired a private tête-a-tête between task force members and select industry leaders. Attended by such notables as Viacom Entertainment chairman Jonathan Dolgen and Sony Pictures Entertainment president Alan J. Levine, as well as Gingrich, the meeting was friendly enough to persuade Bono to scale up his efforts. Still, his initial plan to hold an informal hearing on issues of morality scared off most entertainment executives, requiring a round of late-hour corrective phone calls. "By calling this a hearing," Horowitz told the *Los Angeles Times*, "it brought Whitewater, Watergate [and] Irangate to mind."

Then there was the issue of Bono himself. Horowitz told the paper, "Anyone making the transition from entertainment to politics is confronted with an image problem. Some people still don't take Ronald Reagan seriously. Though Sonny is earnest and serious, that picture of him and Cher in those [bobcat vests and Eskimo boots]...is a powerful one." That's where Horowitz and the center came in. As the most vocal conservative media organization in Hollywood, with a paid membership of about 40,000 and climbing, the group was needed to fill seats. "Among other accomplishments," says Bono's spokesperson, Frank Cullen, "the center has broken fresh ground in terms of bringing more conservatives out." He chuckles. "That is in terms of bringing them into a position where they're not going to be a silent majority, but a participatory majority."

Still, the center, which tends to issue apocalyptic statements to the media, such as "*Showgirls* will be the ultimate test of whether there are any standards left in the modern world," would seem a rather extremist ally for a moderate like Bono. One studio executive later explained his reluctance to attend the meeting in this way: "We wanted Gingrich or Dole or some sign that this was a serious effort. What we were offered was a sideshow created to give Horowitz and his cronies a classier than usual opportunity to mouth off. No thanks." Still, say Republican insiders, the center is pretty much the only conservative game in town, and when you're trying to open doors previously closed, you use whatever crowbar you've got.

The doors to the meeting itself were closed to the press and public, in hopes of loosening participants' lips, underscoring the high stakes of this first exchange between Republicans and Hollywood executives. The strategy seemed to help since, on the eve of the event, a number of entertainment bigwigs had supposedly agreed to attend. Reporters were allowed in only for a brief press conference at the meeting's conclusion, during which everyone thanked each other for attending and Bono took questions.

Surprisingly, given his current position as head of the task force, Bono's credits include his costarring role in *Hairspray*, a film directed by John Waters, whose oeuvre includes at least two films—*Pink Flamingos* and *Female Trouble*—that epitomize everything Dole and Horowitz revile. It would be natural to assume that these experiences had given Bono a finely tuned understanding of aesthetics. And that it might be this very ability that would make him a perfect spokesperson for both Republican views and Hollywood values.

In fact, the mention of these films made Bono visibly uncomfortable. At the suggestion that he's in a unique position to help people like Dole understand the difference between a stylish, subversive film like *Pulp Fiction* and a crowd-pleasing piece of product like *Die Hard With a Vengeance*, Bono answered, "You're right, and I hope I can do that." The complete absence of non-Republican artists from the meeting was noted. "Meetings with artists would be a good second step," he said. "And I would be willing to do that." Does the quirkiness of his resume make life in the House of Representatives rather sticky? "Anyone who thinks life isn't full of conflicts is kidding himself," he answered.

Playing the middleman requires a talent for reading the nuances of behavior, and Bono possesses it, to some degree at least. John Waters remembers Bono's amiability. "On the set, he was a totally lovely man. Not an ounce of trouble. He got along great with Divine and Debbie Harry and everybody. I haven't seen him in years, and I don't know what his politics are now. All I can say is that when I worked with him, he was a kind, gentle man. A real team player." The question is whether under Bono's nerdy geniality there's enough intellectual organization to allow him to interface successfully between the Republican Party, with its abstract moral concerns, and an industry whose values move herdlike behind the dollar.

The day after the meeting the only scoop the *Los Angeles Times* revealed was that everyone who attended agreed that censorship isn't the answer to politicians' complaints about content. When Richard Poirier, communications director of the L.A. County Republican Party, is reached, he sounds positively conciliatory: "We're not calling for censorship," he says. "Take Europe, for example. There's a greater exposure to so-called gratuitous sex and violence in their culture, yet their society is no more violent than ours. The artistic community just reflects what goes on in society. People get a little too sensitive about what young people should or should not be allowed to see. I think young people deserve more respect as individuals." Bob Dole be damned.

Hilary Rosen, president of the Recording Industry Association of America, sees the effort as long overdue. "Regardless of these guys' social agendas, which personally I completely disagree with," she says, "you have to pay attention when government officials are saying that your business is important to them."

But perhaps Lionel Chetwynd, an affable Emmy award-winning screenwriter and producer who heads the Wednesday Morning Club, a conservative think tank based in Beverly Hills, said it best when he paused for reporters outside the meeting. Jokey and with a slightly logy, Rodney Dangerfield-ish energy, he was refreshingly candid off the record. But characteristic of the air of restraint in Hollywood, he kept throwing out witty asides and then retracting them, because "I have to work in this town." Finally, he said, "Look, it's always the same. Republicans are interested in the needs of the industrial heads. Democrats care about the artists. What's going on in there is nothing new, and to think otherwise would be frivolous. But it's a relief. There's a dialogue. And as far as Bono is concerned, well, he's..." And Chetwynd's face struggled valiantly against a bad case of the smirks. "He's doing...well, the best job he is capable of doing." Then his eyes pleaded with us to change the subject.

The secret is that Bono may be the only Republican politician capable of doing this particular job. This is a man who, faced with life's conflicts, has always been able to resolve the paradoxes by projecting at least two personae at once. When Sonny and Cher were releasing soft hippie records and dressing in countercultural garb, Bono was perfectly content to be read on the surface as something he was not sure he was—a threat to the status quo. When he did stand up for what he believed, say in his 1967 psychedelic solo LP *Inner Visions*, a vaguely confessional, antidrug polemic, it was with a certain middle-of-the-road passivity. To quote one of the album's more pointed lyrics, "Inside outside upside down/Everything is turning around/Smell the air it's real uptight/I just sit there." Spoken like a real rolling stone. Like a team player. Sonny Bono's inoffensiveness made him a lousy hippie, but it just may secure him a place in the intransigencies of politics. And the beat goes on.

Real Personal

From the air, Austin, Texas, looks like a toy train set, but without the train. The trees are a little too pretty, too...organized. Buildings, most of them the color of fresh sandcastles, poke cutely through the foliage. The landscape is beige and very flat in all directions. Everything looks faded, I guess on account of the sunlight, which is fierce. It's early July. Texas is in the middle of an unusually long heatwave. One hundred degrees, according to a flight attendant. No joke. Waiting outside the airport a few minutes later, eyes peeled for Bob Mould's silver Subaru, I'm forced to do a little war dance to keep the soles of my tennis shoes from merging with the sidewalk.

Last time I saw Mould, his band, Sugar, was whizzing through Los Angeles on its *Beaster* mini-tour. He and I had recently become friendly, and I was hanging out backstage at the Palladium, trying to act cool, as a succession of alternative-rock gods—Michael Stipe, Evan Dando, and Frank Black among them—dropped by the dressing room to pay their respects. Mould is one of the most honest, bullshit-free, unpretentious people you'll ever meet, but it's hard not to feel humbled around him. I'm not sure why. I mean, it's totally natural to feel indebted to someone whose work helped define your belief and emotions, like Mould and Hüsker Dü did mine. But even Stipe, who's known the guy for more than a decade and is no artistic slouch himself, acted all shy and fidgety, crouching before Mould's folding chair like an acolyte, asking sweet fan-style questions. And Frank Black, who looks a little like Mould crossed with a character out of Peanuts, literally toed the floor and blushed as the two compared touring horror stories.

"Hey!" It's Mould's slightly twangy Midwestern accent. He waves me inside his car, then steers for the 'burbs. "How about this heat, huh?" Wearing his usual faded, untucked T-shirt and loose jeans, Mould is a kind of ageless everyman. He's over six feet tall, with a pale, round face, blue eyes, and short, fine, reddish-blond hair.

"Do you know them?" It takes me a few seconds to recognize the wheezy, ironic, heartbroken tones of Sebadoh issuing from his tape deck.

Great band, I say, nodding at a speaker.

"Yeah, I'm hoping maybe we can hook up with them for a West Coast tour this fall."

Makes sense.

"Yeah," he says, maybe with a slight uncertainty.

You should produce a record for them, I say.

"Oh, I don't know. Producing is okay, but think about it this way. Pick out an album that you liked marginally when it came out, then got totally sick of. Imagine having to listen to nothing but that record for two months. You have to be pretty selective."

Turn a lot of people down?

"I get a lot of offers. From Crosby, Stills, & Nash to—I was supposed to do the latest Lush album. But I had to back out because they sent me a tape of all the material, and I kept choosing the wrong girl's songs." He laughs. "I had to get out before I broke up the band. No, I think I'll stick around here for a while, thanks."

Mould has lived in Austin for a little over a year now, after a couple of years in Brooklyn and Jersey City. With his friend Kevin O'Neill, he cohabits a roomy Mission-style brick house in central Austin, north of the University. Once this house formed the centerpiece of a gargantuan ranch, complete with lake, crops, horses. Long ago subdivided into a woodsy neighborhood, the property is still substantial enough to hold, in addition to the main house, a two-story guest quarters wherein Mould is building a recording studio, and a small pond, recently dug by O'Neill and packed with belching bullfrogs. The main house's interior is dark and cozy, a stained-wood maze with large room and high-ceilinged hallways. The furniture is elegantly nondescript. The stereo is no great shakes, and its turntable is busted. There a few very untrendy figurative paintings on the walls, some of them by friends like singer-songwriter Vic Chesnutt, others selected from O'Neill's modest collection of works by southern "outsider" artists.

We plop down at the dining room table, absorbing the first icy tickles from a rattling AC. Mould leans way over, rubbing the stomach of their scruffy dog, Domino. O'Neill, a slender, handsome, preppily dressed blond, appears with coffee and samples of the cover art for Sugar's new album, which have just arrived via FedEx. We pass them around. Mould and O'Neill are bemused by the eccentric, knick-knacky design—a soft, cartoony pattern that would-n't look inappropriate on the walls of some hipster's kitchen. Mould chose it precisely because it's the last thing people will expect from Sugar, especially after *Beaster*'s sinister cover shot of a bloody, coiled rope.

Strangely enough, it suits the new album just fine. *File Under: Easy Listening*, Sugar's third LP, sounds positively cheery. It may be the happy-go-luckiest batch of songs Mould has penned since Hüsker Dü's *Flip Your Wig* in the mid-'80s. After the tormented beauty of *Copper Blue* and *Beaster*, the lightness of new songs such as "Granny Cool" and "Gee Angel" feels victorious, not to mention hard-won. Does it follow, I wonder, that Mould's feeling A-OK these days?

"Well, I felt pretty good when I wrote those songs." Mould, who laughs easily, gives a tense chuckle. And his hands knot together in his lap.

But not anymore?

He shoots O'Neill a very complicated glance. Maybe O'Neill shoots back an equally complicated glance. "Nope," says Mould. And they both laugh.

Turns out that *FU:EL* almost didn't happen. The first

recording sessions last spring at an Atlanta studio were so unsatisfactory that Mould broke them off, flew back to Austin, and half considered disbanding Sugar. He's still not sure what went wrong. But after a couple of intercontinental phone powwows, the trio reconvened in another studio, and this time everything clicked. Still, Mould remains unnerved and often depressed by this first serious stumbling block in Sugar's short history.

And there's been some fallout. A recent solo appearance at London's Royal Albert Hall—part of a celebration of ten years of Alan McGee's maverick Creation label, which puts out Sugar's records in Britain—turned into something of a psychodrama when Mould's low spirits clashed with the event's pressures to party down, leading to a performance so intense and erratic that some English critics fretted about the state of his mental health in print. This "funk," as he describes it, has yet to lift. Rykodisc, Sugar's American label, thinks *FU:EL* could be a commercial breakthrough, but Mould reports this bit of good news with a shrug. *Copper Blue*, which sold extremely well, achieved success over such a long period of time that it never actually entered Billboard's Top 200, and things never got too crazy on a publicity-fame level. But *FU:EL* could easily enter the charts in the Top 50, if not higher, and Mould can only imagine the hell that could result. All that promotion, all those overtly personal questions, etc....Does it make him think about Kurt Cobain?

"Yeah," he says, spacing out into a sad, sad look. "I wonder if Kurt ever wanted the fame. Or whether he wasn't just caught in this industry that feeds on frail, emotional people."

Did he know Cobain well?

"No, not really. We talked. But his death was definitely a shock, a big letdown. God, that was rough." And Mould looks at O'Neill. "Did I ever tell you that I was originally approached to produce *Nevermind?*" And he looks at me.

No way.

"Mm-hmm." Mould laughs. "Obviously, it didn't happen. But had it happened, well, Nevermind would have been a very different sounding record, I'll tell you."

Less clean?

"A lot less clean."

Things might have gone a lot more sanely for Nirvana.

"Maybe. Who knows? But anyway, back to what you were saying about people confusing an artist's work with his life..." He smiles thinly. "Are you referring to the Hüsker Dü shit?"

"Partly." Like a lot of other Mould fans I know, I had mistakenly assumed that the songs on *Copper Blue* were about ex-Hüsker Dü drummer, Grant Hart. That assumption was contingent on another rather common assumption that Hart and he had been lovers at the time of Hüsker Dü's breakup. But that was before I knew Mould very well, and when I finally got around to testing this interpretation on him, he'd been completely astonished.

"Yeah, that's fucking bizarre," Mould says, remembering our conversation. "That's one I'd never heard before. Not even on the Internet."

Everybody I know thinks they were an item.

"Nope, not at all. Grant wishes." He laughs uproariously. "I'm kidding. Look, I've always wanted people to have the freedom to make the ultimate interpretation of my songs, whether it's something as bizarre as, 'Oh, Bob is writing songs about Grant because he's still upset about the breakup of Hüsker Dü,' or whether it's the people who come up to Kevin and say, 'I saw you having coffee with Bob. Are his songs about you?'" Mould lets out another huge laugh. "Kevin always says, 'Hey, do you think I'd be having coffee with Bob if those songs were about me?'"

I guess that's one of the pitfalls of keeping your mouth shut.

"Maybe. When Hüsker Dü broke up, I jut stayed out of it. I let Grant say what he was going to say, and I didn't weigh in. I had a lot of personal stuff to figure out.

Ultimately, who knows what happened? I'd gotten sober, someone else in the band hadn't. There were a lot of things. But the only song I had ever written that's had anything directly to do with the breakup of Hüsker Dü is 'The Poison Years.' At least that I know of. But...Grant and I as lovers? That's too much."

And while we're demystifying you, you weren't a junkie either?

"I wasn't a junkie," he repeats. "Heroin wasn't my problem. Drinking and speed. Speed really ate a hole in me, and it's still there. It's permanent." He raises his hand and looks at the back, the palm. "You can see right through it."

Mould knows that I'm going to get around to the issue of his sexual preference. In the last year especially, he's begun to be outed in print—in zines, in gay periodicals, and even in a few mainstream magazines. Just two days earlier, I'd questioned a British journalist friend's plan to mention Mould's homosexuality in a forthcoming magazine article. She just rolled her eyes, saying he was already out in England.

Last fall, Mould and I had discussed how I might handle the topic if I ever got the opportunity to write about him. Well, here we are, and it's a far more difficult and complex moment than gay activists would have you believe. Like Mould, I have doubts about both the importance of these kinds of self-labeling pronouncements and the public's right to know. But there's fierce external pressure on Mould to acknowledge his sexuality in a clear way, and he wants to get it over with so that Sugar and he can do what they do. So, since we're already on the topic of demystification, I wonder aloud if it's time to make the leap.

"Yeah, I guess we can. But let's eat first." He looks at O'Neill, who has been watching Mould with his usual tender concern. "You hungry?"

O'Neill nods furiously.

We hop in the Subaru, blast the AC, crank the Sebadoh, and head to Threadgill's, a legendary local eatery with an eccentric, faux-Americana decor and a menu huge enough to accommodate both O'Neill's vegetarianism and Mould's meaty diet. Some of the younger patrons recognize Mould as soon as we walk in. Their mouths stop moving and one or two people point, but no one approaches, and he seems oblivious and relaxed.

As serious as Mould can be, he's also a lot of fun, not to mention a great storehouse of (unconfirmed) information and gossip about the rock world. Over the course of our roughly hour-long meal he: (1) breaks the bad news that his brilliant, finicky friend Kevin Shields of My Bloody Valentine has just scrapped MBV's long-awaited, nearly completed new album, (2) acknowledges the existence of secret sound recordings, made by an acquaintance, on which Kurt Cobain and Courtney Love allegedly are heard having intense, unflattering (to her) shouting matches, and (3) describes recording studio troubles on the Butthole Surfers front that make *FU:EL*'s difficult birth seem trivial.

But before you deduce that deep down, under all that integrity, Mould is a just another excitable rumormonger, you need to hear the horrified tone of his gossiping. One of Mould's favorite words is "information." He talks a lot about the importance of the complete picture, and how the media amorally distort and eroticize information under the guise of telling all. Another of his favorite words, at least during this visit, is "freak." He uses it to describe self-imposed victims of culture's information mania. Specifically some of his peers—the Farrells, Dandos, Loves, et al.—are intelligent folk and true artists whom he sees as behaving like rock 'n' roll cartoons in a desperate attempt to snag the media's limited attention span. "Freak" is what he's afraid of becoming, should the media discover some reducible, exploitable part of his personality. And homosexuality appears to be their idea of that long-awaited hook.

But, well, Mould can explain all this far better than I can. And after a quick stop at his favorite local record store to buy the new Guided by Voices EP, we streak home so he can do just that. O'Neill, who handles Sugar's business affairs, retires to a room just off the kitchen. Mould gives Domino a few stomach rubs. Then he and I head to the den, pull up two chairs to the coffee table, and warily study the tiny skyscraper of my microcassette recorder.

"Okay, let's go for it." Mould blinks at the recorder's red light, then sits back in his chair, and looks off into the distance. "Well," he says, "It seems that a lot of publications are hovering around, expecting some kind of grand statement about my sexuality. I don't think it's any kind of secret within the music industry and within the fan base at large what my sexual preference is. But this year it seems to be a gigantic issue. You know, 'Bob, it's time for you to come out and represent the gay community.' Or, 'Bob, it's time for you to be a role model because you are a successful artist who has transcended your 'affliction,' your 'stigma,' your...' something that I had fucking nothing to do with. I was born with it. My life is no different than anyone else's. People are going to have to get over the fact that I prefer not to talk about my sexual preference, nor do I really care about reading about anyone else's sexual preference. Because everybody on this earth, as far as I know, has a sexual preference. And if people are going to continually come to me looking for some kind of description, whether it be philosophical or sordid in nature, well..." And his eyes kind of charge.

"I am not a fucking freak." He looks at me. "I'm not going to be paraded around like a freak. I don't like the word 'gay' because I don't know what the word really means. The fact that I'm supposed to make outrageous statements to gain more column space in music publications is insulting. And if the gay community doesn't like it, then too fucking bad. I'm not your spokesperson, because

I don't know what you're about. I'm a person, a human being. I'm an artist. I write songs. I'm a storyteller. I don't think, 'Hey, is it time to write a happy gay pop song, or is it time to write a depressing gay pop songs?" Who the fuck sits down to think about that shit? Who in their right mind thinks like that? I don't. I expect to be judged on how I treat other people and how I carry myself as a human being. I do not flaunt my sexuality. I do not deny my sexuality. It is my sexuality. It is not the public's sexuality. It is none of their fucking business. I don't do what I do for some flag that I'm supposed to wave, I do it for Bob. People better get over that. I'm not a fucking freak. Or at least not because of that. I might be a freak for other reasons, because I'm a control freak, because of my compulsive behavior, because of my character flaws. But not because of that."

Anybody who really knows his work, I say, won't be surprised by his discomfort at the idea of being labeled.

"I am an island." Mould laughs. "And I like it that way."

I'd argue that the really oppressed people in American society circa 1994 are individuals like Mould who feel confined by the notion of collective identity.

"I'm not questioning my sexuality," Mould says. "That's never been a question in my whole life, for as long as I can remember. What I'm questioning is, am I supposed to be the cause célèbre for something I don't understand? And I know there are a lot of conflicts in what I'm saying. I know there are a lot of people who are going to hate this and say, 'Oh Bob, what a fucking loser. This is such bullshit. What a cop-out.' Well, I've been writing songs since I was nine years old. And I don't feel like I have to turn a very unimportant sidebar in my life into a headline just to compete with all the other freaks. And listen, if people don't like it, ultimately, they can fuck off. They can rot in hell."

Does he think the fascination with his sexuality is part of the larger trend of people substituting intense, mythical, media-controlled relationships with troubled celebrities for, well, real relationships?

"Sure. Kerrigan and Harding, O.J. Simpson, the Menendezes...none of these stories really speak to anyone, do they? They don't speak to me anyway. All these alleged tragic figures. What are people really absorbing from these spectacles? What's the information here? If this is what the world's coming to, then everything is just about a freak alert."

He shakes his head. "Society is losing its grip. It's like, we don't have the circus anymore. We don't have the He-She, the Dog Boy. Instead we have a bunch of people trying to cop this psychotherapy babble to sell records. Like this 'I'm clean when I'm really using dope' concept. Issue after issue of every magazine is just thriving on it. Magazines are in the industry of supporting the industry, let's not kid ourselves. It's not about the value of your work anymore, it's about the sordid details of your private life. There's no sanctity. Well, listen, I've go nothing to hide, but there are some things that are mine and only mine. I think I give people more than enough of my things. But there are some things that belong just to me."

Rebel Just Because

Leonardo DiCaprio walks into the Dresden Room, a semi-legendary bar and restaurant in the East Hollywood district of Los Feliz. He's here to promote two films, *William Shakespeare's Romeo and Juliet* and *Marvin's Room*, both in release this fall. That's two movies to add to a catalog of credits that grew from a mid-'80s TV stint on *Growing Pains* into an Oscar nomination for *What's Eating Gilbert Grape?* He's wearing a faded red T-shirt, loose blue jeans, running shoes, and has a girl's barrette in his hair. He's six feet tall, lanky, thin but fleshy, and moves rapidly with a wary, teenaged lope. He looks like a very large adolescent boy with weirdly knowing, nervous eyes. When I wave, he crashes down at my table, orders a 7-Up, and immediately bums a Camel Lite Wide off of me. He's friendly, reserved, and very focused. He has a flat, affectless L.A. accent and a mid-range crackly voice with a sardonic edge. He's talkative, easily bemused, and very well mannered. In other words, he is nothing like what I'd expected, i.e. a mischievous brat.

After spending two hours with DiCaprio, first doing the interview, then just hanging out talking about this and that, it's hard to imagine how all the wild rumors about him got started. For instance, just a month before the interview, a friend told me he'd heard that DiCaprio had raped a girl and it was being covered up. Then another friend told me he'd heard that the rape story was a plant to hide the fact that the actor is gay. He's supposedly been in and out of rehab, is a recent convert to Scientology, and I forget what else. People seem absolutely determined to make him into the new River Phoenix. You know, tormented, unstable, brilliant, self-destructive. When you meet him, all that seems so absurd. To me he seems like a sweet, canny, clear-headed, sane, young heterosexual guy—fun-loving but a little sad and anxious, intelligent and highly insecure about his intelligence—who likes going to art museums, loves his family, hated all the summer blockbuster movies, adores acting, and dreams of swimming with blue whales. Why people insist on projecting all the gloom and doom onto him, I don't know. But I was determined not to perpetuate the myths. So I began the interview at square one.

DENNIS COOPER: In almost every article I've ever read about you, journalists ask the same questions, and make the same presumptions. You know, that you're a party animal, that you have drug problems, that you're gay and closeted, that you're a brat...

LEONARDO DICAPRIO: Yeah, they are all kind of the same.

It always seems like journalists treat you fair and square when they're with you, but then, when they actually write the articles, they start speculating and drooling all over you.

[Laughs] Yeah.

I guess that *Details* cover story on you last year was the most notorious.

That guy...I was really nice to him. I brought him over to my house, and introduced him to my mom, and then he twisted things around to make me seem like a bad-ass, when it wasn't like that at all.

Everyone I know thought the piece was creepy. Well, I'm going to try to not cover the same old ground, and if I get creepy, you can be a bad-ass and throw your Coke in my face.

[Laughs] OK.

Supposedly one can tell a lot about someone by what they find funny, so tell me a joke.

I just heard some good ones. Let me think. [Pause] OK. A guy hears a knock on his door. He answers it. There's nobody there, but he looks down and sees a snail. So he picks up the snail and throws it as far as he can. Three years later there's a knock on the door. He answers it, and there's this snail. And the snail says, "What the fuck was that about?" [both laugh] You tell me one.

This one's kind of old, but...What were Kurt Cobain's last words?

I don't know.

Hole's gonna be big.

[Laughs] That's pretty sick.

Well, something has just been revealed about you, but I'm not sure what it is. So, I just saw a chunk of *Romeo and Juliet,* sort of a montage of scenes. From what I could tell, it looked amazing. Have you seen the film?

I saw a rough cut. Yeah, it looks pretty wild.

Did you see *Trainspotting?*

That's a great movie. I loved that movie.

Both movies are based on literary works that are very dense and complex on the page, and they both make this savvy decision to neutralize the difficulties of the language by being incredibly stylized and energetic. It seemed like a great way to deal with Shakespeare.

Yeah. Some people have criticized the movie. You know, "You can't do that to Shakespeare. You shouldn't mess with Shakespeare like that." But Shakespeare was a genius. I'm sure if he was alive he would have been totally behind what [director] Baz [Luhrmann] is trying to do. And I see what you mean about the two movies. But Baz didn't see *Trainspotting* until a few weeks ago, so it's just a coincidence.

The movie has that wacky, surreal Australian feel, á la *Priscilla* or *Muriel's Wedding.*

But it's not like that, really. It's definitely surreal, but...

The black drag queen with the white afro?

That's Mercutio. That's at the ball where Romeo meets Juliet. Romeo's on drugs, and that's him tripping out on Mercutio. Mercutio's wearing the afro as part of his costume, but I trip out on him, and it grows about three feet. That's a wild scene. In this version, the ball takes place at a club, and everybody's on drugs and dancing. It's crazy. But the movie's very real, too. I don't know how to explain it. You just have to see it.

Romeo's a tricky one. He's so lovey dovey. In the Zeffirelli version, the way Leonard Whiting played him, he was such a bland, wussy guy.

Yeah. Well, at first I wasn't sure about doing this. I didn't want to run around in tights swinging a sword, you know? But Baz convinced me to come to Australia and meet with him for a week, and while I was there he figured out what his vision was, and then I was really interested.

Is Romeo still a total innocent in this version?

He's pretty innocent. Well, in the first half he is. Then Mercutio dies and Tybalt dies, and everything just goes wrong. I'm crying all the time in the last half of the film. I cry a lot in this movie. That was hard.

You filmed in Mexico City. Is it as hellish a place as one hears?

Well, while we were making the movie, somebody on the crew got attacked, and somebody else got robbed, and somebody else got shot. And they say Mexico City has the worst smog of any city in the world. But it was nice too, because it's not a place where tourists tend to go. It's kind of undiscovered in that sense. And some people I know from New York were down, so that was fun. There's a lot of poverty, and that was depressing, but there are parts of the city that are just like Beverly Hills.

Are there good clubs there?

There are some clubs. But we didn't do that so much. We were more into silver.

Silver?

[Grins] Silver.

In what sense?

We got into buying silver. You can buy these bracelets and necklaces and things, and these guys will etch your name into them, or these skulls. We'd go out in the city wearing all this silver and people thought we were just ridiculous. [Laughs] I haven't worn them out here, but they're nice to have, you know?

What kind of music do you like?

I like rap. Nas, Wu Tang, that sort of thing.

Are you political?

Not really. I try to stay out of that because it's so damn confusing. I sort of want Clinton, because I don't think he's that bad. [Laughs] He seems like a nice-guy President.

Are you religious?

Haven't been brought up that way. But I have a weird karma thing. Like I used to be able to steal bubble gum and stuff when I was younger, but I'm really ridiculous with it now. If someone gives me the wrong change, I can't deal with it, even if it's a gigantic department store. It's not because I'm getting money now. It's because I always think that when I go outside, something terrible is going to happen.

All that, and you're not interested in Buddhism?

My brother is, and he's constantly preaching to me. I'm curious about it. I want to get into it, but I want to know a lot more about it. But, yeah, I'd say it was the best religion. [Laughs] There I go with my big thing: "Yeah, I'd say Buddhism is the best religion." [Laughs] In bold print.

Here's a hypothetical for you. A friend posed this to me. Would you rather be really, really fat or really, really old?

You mean old-looking?

No, old. Either you're 95 years old or you're your age and weigh 500 pounds.

I'd be really fat, and go out like Biggie Smalls every night, you know what I'm saying? I'd have people wheel me into places. I'd have a woman on each leg. I'd go out like a rock star if I was that big. Yeah, I'd rather be fat. I mean...really old? Man.

I found the question harder to answer than you did.

Maybe because I'm older than you are.

Well, I did *Gilbert Grape,* and Mama was pretty big, but she was just the sweetest woman that I have ever met in my entire life. I still talk to her every once in a while. And I have a friend who's...pretty large, and who I hang out with every day, and he's the sweetest guy ever. I really like to have sweet people around me. I can't stand bad-asses. There's too many of them, especially my age in L.A. I like to get to know people, and you have to peel away so many layers of those people. Just give me someone who's relaxed and cool to hang out with, even if they're not studs.

Well, you being you, a lot of people want to be your pal.

I have a good group of friends, people I've accumulated over the years. Some I've known since elementary school, some I've met recently. They're just a good group of guys and gals. And I think they like me too.

But you're never sure.

You're never sure. No, I know they like me. Because it's not really about that, you know? Our friendships are completely separate from everything else. I hardly know anybody who's...in show biz. It seems like I do through all the press, but I really don't.

So is it difficult for you when you attend say the Cannes Film Festival or something? You know, flash-flash-flash.

I'm great at avoiding press, too. [Laughs] I've been handling this thing pretty well. I keep thinking something bad is going to happen, but it's been pretty cool so far. I've maintained the exact same home life that I've had for 20 years. All I see is more people looking at me than before, but, you know, who cares? You just can't obsess yourself with this fame stuff. I used to take everything to heart. When the things they said to me in the press were detrimental, I thought it would kill me. But stuff keeps changing all the time, and now I'm cool about it, and I just think it's weird to watch it all happen.

I get the feeling that *Total Eclipse,* about the relation-

ship between the French poets Rimbaud and Verlaine, was a rather discomfiting experience for you. It wasn't very well liked.

People hated it.

I'm one of the only people I know who thought the film was interesting. But then I love Rimbaud. When I was a teenager, Rimbaud was my hero. He's still my hero, in a way.

Really? That's cool. Yeah, I wanted to do the part because Rimbaud was such a bad-ass, but he was a genius, so he had the goods to back it up, you know? I think the only people who liked *Total Eclipse* were people who liked Rimbaud. But then, a lot of people who liked Rimbaud hated it too. I don't really know what to say about *Total Eclipse*. The movie was made in France. Over there, Rimbaud's like James Dean, but over here people really don't know who he is. And I think maybe the film didn't explain enough.

The way people reacted to the film, you'd have thought the whole movie was just a frame around the scene where you and David Thewlis, who plays Verlaine, kiss.

I know, I know. It was crazy.

And *Total Eclipse* came right on the heels of *The Basketball Diaries*, another film nobody liked very much.

Yep. But you know what? It doesn't really bother me what people think.

Before those movies came out, you were seen as the brilliant young actor, the Academy Award nominee, and then suddenly you were the actor everybody gossiped about. You were supposedly a junkie, and you were gay. Assuming that neither one of those rumors is true, that had to have bothered you.

Sure. But I'm really glad I did those movies. I'm proud of my work in them. In five years nobody will remember any of that, or the bad reviews, and my work in them will be seen as part of all of my work. I'm not worried about that. I just think people expected me to go a certain way with my career, and I didn't do it. I didn't do the next John Grisham movie.

Did it make you gun-shy?

No. I want to keep doing different things. But I want to say this: I don't do drugs. I've never done drugs in my life. I'm just not interested. And if any of my friends start doing drugs, they're going to hear about it from me. What people don't realize is that half of the reason I did *The Basketball Diaries* is because of the whole heroin craze, and...I'm not saying I was doing a "Say No to Drugs" special or anything, but I wanted to help make some kind of statement against heroin. But then, of course, people decide I'm into it, right? God damn. And I also want to say that I've had a girlfriend for a year coming up. I'm sure people will make something out of that.

It's amazing to me, what with all the rumors about you, that you trust people at all.

I don't, really. Like I had a friend who I did a short film with recently who slandered me. I was trying to do a favor for him. His name's R.D. Robb. It's scandalous. It was originally a short film, and then he tried to make it into a feature. I worked one night on it. He tried to make it into a feature. And I heard all this stuff about how he was going to pit the press against me if I didn't go along with him and do the feature. I just did it as a favor, you know? And then all this stuff happens and you ask why. Why be nice if that's going to happen?

The editor of *Detour* wanted me to ask you about something. Answer or not as you see fit.

Let me guess, sex and drugs.

Well, you tell me. In *Vanity Fair*, Alicia Silverstone is asked about you, and there's an implication that you and she were romantically involved at some point, and she says something on the order of, "I don't even want to talk about that guy," meaning you. So...

Right. [Sighs] Alicia and I did our first movies at about the same time. We've known each other for years. We're not really good friends or anything, but we know each other. I'm sure she was asked that question, and she thought it was ridiculous, and she just said, "I'm not even going to answer that question," just like I would do.

You've played two brilliant young writers, Rimbaud and Jim Carroll. I'm wondering if the way you think about acting is in any way related to the way they thought about writing.

Hmm. I wish I could come up with a brilliant answer to that, but I can't.

An actor I know told me that for him, acting was like being in a trance.

I've heard people say that. I never took acting lessons, so I don't have a way to think about it like that. I know some actors get sort of lost in what they're doing. I'm not like that. I like to know everything that's going on around me. I guess when I'm acting, I think of myself as the camera. I'm watching myself act. I'm trying to see how what I'm doing looks from the outside.

That's interesting. It seems like it would make you feel really self-conscious.

I feel self-conscious all the time anyway.

After *Total Eclipse* and *The Basketball Diaries,* you're seen as a real risk-taker. You must get a lot of weird scripts.

You're right, I do. But I don't mind. I'm always looking for something different.

Did you know John Waters wrote a film thinking of you for the lead? It was called *Cecil B. Demented,* and you would have played an avant-garde Super-8 filmmaker who kidnaps a major movie star and forces her to star in his Super-8 film. But the film didn't happen for whatever reason.

Yeah. I had dinner with John a couple of weeks ago at [photographer] Greg Gorman's. He's one of the people who's really doing it, and I admire him a lot. And he's just hilarious. He tells the best stories.

John's the best. So do you have any small, risky films in the works?

I have one thing in the works, but we'll see.

Is that *The Inside Man?* You initiated that project, didn't you?

It's not my project. It's just...this project came along, and I really liked it, and I took it to Michael Mann because I loved *Heat.* He's such an intelligent guy. He's like a computer, he knows so much. So he's interested, and it's in the works, and we'll see. I don't really want to talk too much about it right now. But I have this huge movie coming up.

James Cameron's *Titanic.*

Yeah.

You seem a little nervous about it.

No, I just...I've never done anything like this. I never planned to do a movie like this, but I agreed to do it, and...it should be interesting. It's a huge movie, like I said. Huge. One-hundred-twenty-million-dollar budget, and a six-month shoot. Jim Cameron says he wants it be a *Doctor Zhivago* type of thing, and it'll be interesting to be part of that. It's an epic love story that goes backwards and forwards in time.

Do you go down with the ship?

[Nods] Dead.

Cameron's films are generally amazing things, but I don't think of his films as places where actors get to shine very much. It's more like they become parts of the machinery. But maybe *Titanic* won't be so special-effects oriented.

Phew. It is. Huge special effects. I don't know, I'm just going to do it, and we'll see.

I've read that you love to travel.

I do. I just skydived recently. My 'chute didn't open. [Laughs]

Well, you're here.

Yeah, I'm here. It was a tandem thing, and I jumped out of the plane, and I pulled the cord, and my 'chute didn't open. And the next thing I know, the guy with me pulls out a knife and cuts this cord and we start free-falling. And you know, it's not like a video game where if you mess up, you're OK, you lose a quarter. [Laughs] This is your life. The whole trip down I didn't cry. I wasn't weirded-out by it. I was just...depressed. [Laughs] Let's see, this year I also went scuba diving in the Great Barrier Reef.

I've always wanted to do that.

Oh, God. It's like space. It's the best thing you could ever do. Better than anything.

I saw the IMAX film about it.

Yeah, the one Meryl Streep narrates. That was trippy. Did you see that ill sea creature that was at the bottom of the ocean that was about a mile long? How trippy was that, bro? [Laughs] When I was young, I had this thing where I wanted to see everything. It's weird how that's sort of died down. I used to think, How can I die on this earth without seeing every inch of this world?

Have you been a lot of places?

I have. Madagascar is where I really want to go next. I went to Africa for *Total Eclipse,* but I didn't see any wildlife at all. It was depressing. We shot between Somalia and Ethiopia, which is where all the refugees go, so it was like...kids walking around on all fours from polio, literally like animals.

Do you ever pick films because they're going to be shot in exotic locales?

Nope. Otherwise I wouldn't have chosen Mexico twice. I'm going to be spending a year of my life in Mexico.

Isn't Titanic being filmed there?

Yeah. Rosarito Beach. There's garbage everywhere.

At least you're in a profession where you get incredible opportunities, like being able to travel a lot.

It is fucking cool. I really love acting. I love it when it's really about acting. I love it when you get to create stuff, and collaborate with a director. You feel like what you're doing is not going to waste. It's in the archives. It's going to be there for years. Pain is temporary, film is forever. That's my big quote that [*This Boy's Life* director] Michael Caton-Jones told me: "Pain is temporary, film is forever."

But then you'll get old and you'll have pain all the time.
Mm-hm I don't know. [Pause] My grandpa just died last year. That was a big depressing thing. And my dog died. Our household dog. Last year was like the year of...misery. But this year, so far, I have to say I'm liking it a lot.

No complaints?
No complaints.

A Raver Runs Through It

(co-written with Joel Westendorf)

Even if you haven't read *On the Road,* you probably know the story of Jack Kerouac and Neal Cassady's semi-mythological road trip. If you don't know the story, suffice to say it took place in the 1950s, a time of political conservatism and pervasive emotional and sexual repression. These two future Beat icons set off in search of what they believed was the real, if temporarily confused, America, a place of unlimited hope and big, wild dreams.

Well, this is that kind of story. Except our wanderlust hasn't been fueled by jazz, booze, and the prismatic beauty of free verse poetry. Instead, it's stoked by rave's dreamy, experimental music and almost crazily sweet ideology. We're heading into a more fucked-up America, with ever more blind faith than the Beats could ever imagine.

O ur rental car is zipping through the huge blur of desert between Palm Springs and the eastern California border. Somewhere beyond the desert's bleak and scalding horizon is Flagstaff, Arizona, site of the World Unity Festival, billed as a weeklong United Nations-sponsored showcase for indigenous cultures from around the world. We're targeting one of the festival's sub-events, a four-day Mega-Rave that has been the talk of rave aficionados since it popped up on the Internet last spring. Supposedly organized by the Zippies, a relentlessly self-hyping gaggle of middle-aged English rave promoters, it promises to do for ravers what the original Woodstock did for the hippie set, namely crystallize an underground movement, magnetize a thus far indifferent media, and give the already converted an incredible time.

The two of us are friends, but we come from very different backgrounds. One (Dennis) was rudely awakened from childhood when an older friend played him *The Velvet Underground and Nico,* and his musical taste has evolved along alternative rock lines ever since. The other (Joel), almost 20 years younger, grew up addicted to soul and R&B, but with enough interest in New Age music to spend his Sundays with a syndicated radio program called "Musical Starstreams." Still, he only fell in love when electronics married tribal rhythms in the sprawling genre dubbed techno. To Dennis, dance music is little more than a form of mass hypnosis. To Joel, rock'n'roll has grown unchallenging and obvious, and Stone Temple Pilots have a cuter feel than Sonic Youth. Point is, we're plunging into rave culture with mixed feelings.

To read published reports in magazines such as *Details* and *Option,* you'd think rave was already dead in its crib, a victim of its proponents' drug-induced befuddlement, and of inter-scene squabbles over what constitutes a pure rave experience. But that contradicts everything we've seen and felt over the past four months as we crisscrossed the western United States and visited rave's hothouse, London. Dennis, whose limited scene experience and indie-rock bent makes him something of a rave couch potato, is feeling a rumble of countercultural hope that he hasn't felt since the early days of punk. Joel's identity has already been shaped by his immersion in rave culture, and he talks excitedly about his and his friends' intentions to infect the world with their wide-eyed enthusiasm.

So what is rave exactly? Well, it's hard to explain. You might think back to the mid-'70s, or even further back to the late '60s, in the sense that, like punk and hippiedom, rave is a countercultural movement with specific musical taste, a highly developed fashion sense, and a left-of-Democratic politic. But unlike punks or hippies, ravers are more interested in issues of spiritual growth and increased communication than they are in transgressing traditional political structures. To generalize—and with a movement this amorphous, you're forced to—ravers tend to see the government and its laws as beside the point. If ravers lionize anything, it's technology, which offers ways to circumvent the kinds of blockage that derailed countercultures of the past. Rave is not about destroying corrupt power structures; it's about general things like self-belief, open-mindedness, and faith. It's about seeking the limitless. Hippies and punks named their enemies, which helped the media define them. They had specific goals, and when these goals weren't met, their movements were easily debunked. Ravers have no particular enemies, so they're relatively invisible. And their invisibility is their strength.

Rave is nothing particularly new. In England, the movement has been barreling along since 1987 or before. But in America, where the media tends to grab, misread, and gentrify every passing trend at birth, rave has somehow managed to grow in popularity and mutate aesthetically for a number of years now, with only the occasional sidelong glance from MTV and the rock music press. *Wired* and *Mondo 2000* have done their share of profiles, but, even there, coverage has been light, slanted to suit the magazines' technological themes, and bemusedly parental in tone. Then there articles like the feature in *Details,* which quoted a few disgruntled fans and promoters, then declared the L.A. rave scene a dead duck.

It's kind of ironic that Los Angeles's Millennium I, which quickly sold out its 8,000 tickets, happened just about the time that Details ran its funeral oratory. Organized by local promoters to meet the speculations of film director Kathryn Bigelow, whose movie Strange Days required a huge New Year's Eve 1999 party scene, Millennium I was the exact opposite of an illegal underground party. Heavily advertised on local radio, its location in the streets of downtown Los Angeles required governmental support and massive police protection, which in turn severely curtailed attendees' drug use. A blocked-off intersection at the base of the Bonaventure Hotel became an immense, cross-shaped dance floor, blindingly lit for the cameras, constantly sprayed with confetti, and surrounded by actors dressed as machine-gun-toting National Guardsmen. The rave itself could easily have been dwarfed or coopted by the moviemakers' designs and equipment. Instead they just seemed surreal, a kind of visual drug substitute that meshed surprisingly well with the sound of techno echoing wildly through the skyscrapers. Millennium I felt like a raver invasion. The ecstatic quality of the dancing that night had nothing to do with ecstasy per se, and everything to do with having finally won a long, uphill battle.

So we've made it to Flagstaff. Unlike the bulk of Arizona, which is culturally arid and politically inhospitable, Flagstaff is a pretty little college town buried in the woods about 80 miles from the Grand Canyon's southern rim. Deep in its historic downtown section, currently a scaffold-covered eyesore partway through a Disneyland-style "restoration" project, is the office of the World Unity Festival. Occupying a room on the second floor of an artists' co-op building, its puniness is the first sign that we might be in for a letdown. In the doorway stands a short, balding hippie type, clearly stoned and obviously more than a little stressed out. Behind him several hones ring, ring, ring. He's staring forlornly out a dusty window, but when he spots us, he simultaneously stiffens and breaks into a shit-eating grin.

It seems the festival, scheduled to begin today, is siteless at the moment, not to mention long abandoned by the United Nations. The original site, near the Canyon, was never officially okayed. The second site, on a nearby Indian reservation, was yanked just two days ago when tribal leaders realized the scale of the planned event. But there's a chance, he says, that a local hippie commune, the Turtle Family, might donate part of its property, although he's not advising people to head on up there just yet since the roads to the commune are currently blocked off by police and their drug-sniffing dogs. "Check back later this afternoon," he tells us. Uh, will do. But in the meantime, how do we get in touch with the Zippies? He looks at us blankly. You know, the people who are organizing the Mega-Rave? His bloodshot eyes widen. "The...what?"

On the street, we buy a local newspaper. Sure enough, its front page is a multipart article detailing the festival organizers' incompetence. There are several pictures of despondent out-of-towners slouched in front of local businesses and wandering the streets. We drive around he city, blasting techno, the place a sea of lost festival-goers. Every once in a while, a car will pass ours, also blasting techno, and hopeful squints are exchanged. Plastikman is in the tape deck. Joel is dancing in his seat, head flicking back and forth, his hands raised, fingers slicing at the air. Dennis is constitutionally unsuited to dancing, but he's all ears. Plastikman, a project of a young Canadian named Richie Hawtin, uses a speedy, rolling ticktock beat overlaid with spare, shredded-sounding synthesizer textures. It sounds like a bit like straw feels. Crackly.

We stop into what appear to be Flagstaff's two hippest CD stores; neither of the shop's clerks have heard anything about a Mega-Rave, and don't seem particularly interested in the prospect. So we give up for the moment and check into a hotel, lug our clothes and tapes inside, and settle in for what looks to be a very long week. The Mega-Rave is scheduled to commence two days from now, so all is not lost quite yet. Still, when we call the Festival office later in the afternoon, the phones have been disconnected, and we reluctantly begin studying the hotel's *Tourist Guide.*

Dennis is pissed. He's used to the rock world's professionalism. After all, rock'n'roll has had decades to organize. But Joel is just a little bit disappointed. He scrunches his face up, and glares into space for a couple of minutes.

Then he's his cheery young self again, leaning over a road map, calculating the distance from here to the town of Sedona, supposedly a site of great spiritual energy. Apparently, fuck-ups like this aren't uncommon in rave culture. Maybe now just isn't the time for a Mega-Rave. Maybe the culture is still too chaotic and lively to get that in focus. So in a way it's a positive thing, eyes on the future and all that. Dennis wonders if Joel's in denial or something. Then he thinks about Woodstock, and how much more interesting '70s rock might have been without that overrated signpost. If nothing else, we might have been spared Ten Years After.

Earlier in the summer we separately attended two rave-related events, one of which piqued Dennis's interest, the other of which confirmed Joel's hopes.

Narnia is the closest thing rave culture has to a Lollapalooza. This yearly rave, always held in some unannounced location in California, has a reputation for being the most elaborate and professional event in the country. Named after a series of novels by C. S. Lewis, it promises a veritable dream world: seven different "lands," one to suit attendees' every possible mood, from an ambient area for relaxing between dance spurts, to a special effects-thrashed area featuring the hardest techno beats. Dennis, being the novice of this duo. figured Narnia was the perfect place to begin.

Narnia, near San Diego, California: At first I don't know where I am. Then my eyes adjust and the place gets real. I'm at the entrance of an abandoned quarry. A dozen huge mounds of gravel and dirt have gradually weathered into a mini-mountain range, creating a series of isolated valleys connected by winding trails. The entirety is lit up in blurry purples, reds, and yellows, and criss-crossed by thousands of vibrating laser beams coming from all directions. They rise and fall every couple of seconds like a thatched lid. Passing through them, I'm bombarded by a confusion of sounds—a soft, meandering whir from a small gravel pit over to my left; some old-fashioned hip hop blasting from a big tin shed over the hill to my right; acid jazz apparently being played live at some spot in the distance; and, overwhelming them all, the *thud-thud-thud* and *squeak-squeak-squeak* of techno pounding from the valley below me.

I wander around, following the little trails from gravel pit to gravel pit. The ambient area has a sleepy, campfire atmosphere. People are scrunched up in sleeping bags, talking and passing joints. Up and over the hill is the acid jazz area. A band plays on an unlit stage, but most of the listeners are gathered at a series of booths along the pit's opposite wall. One booth offers face painting. Greenpeace mans another. Two booths sell legal faux ecstasy pills made from ephedra root, ginseng, and other herbs. I buy a few, then take the first trail I find into a pit full of stuttering white light. The music sounds like a skipping CD. There are several hundred stiffened bodies of indeterminate gender vibrating on their feet in a clump They look like they're being electrocuted. I'm out of here, and over the hill. Which brings me back to techno.

This is obviously Narnia's main attraction. It's easily four times larger than the other pits, and ringed by a long, narrow, curving stage full of drums, gongs, speaker cabinets, and several mixing desks. Above the stage hangs a five-story screen, upon which lasers, slides, and Super-8 movie loops battle it out at such a high speed that it's impossible to pick out the imagery. All around me, thousands of people dance, grin, and stare at the same time. Most of them look very high, but there's not a beer can or bottle to be seen, which may be the most disorienting detail of all. Teenagers and people in their 20s predominate, but there is a fair number of us older types, and, unlike at a rock gig, I can't immediately peg them as record company employees. The male-to-female ratio is about

60:40. Clothes are loose, colorful, and designer casual. Hairstyles vary from hippie-esque to shaved.

It's strange how seductive the music becomes in this setting, even to these rockist's ears. Songs parade by, crossfading almost unnoticeable, like individual movements in some vast, night-long symphony. I stand around for a while, kind of weak in the knees, craning my neck, trying to decide if it's the most otherworldly sight I've ever seen, off acid anyway. Everybody looks intensely self-involved. Their slack, unreadable expressions give the scene its only meaning, though I'm not exactly sure what it means. They just move around in tight little areas, mesmerized by their surroundings, oblivious to but seemingly respectful of their neighbors. One woman is dressed as a butterfly. Anther guy is wearing a space suit. Sometimes they're in sharp silhouette. Sometimes, when the light show cooperates, they're so garishly lit you'd think they were paid entertainers.

They're amazing to watch, better than a band, maybe because they're just a slightly more extroverted fraction of the rest of us—a kind of rave focus group in whose galloping bodies and delirious expressions it's actually possible to see pure, unmitigated happiness, like the kind cartoon characters feel. The music speeds up, slows down, speeds up. The light show flutters through its insane narrative. And I leave, fried, around 4 am, pissed at myself for being such a wallflower, and wondering why my friends and I are so unwilling to really and truly relax.

Joel, whose previous rave experience gives him more access to the subtleties, chose the Rainbow Gathering, again an annual event, this year held a couple of hours south of Yellowstone Park. The Gathering, whose existence long predates rave, has traditionally been a kind of weekend-long camp-out and convocation for hippies and Deadheads, but it's become a popular place for ravers to meet and exchange ideas about the future of their movement.

The Rainbow Gathering, Wyoming: Last year the 23rd annual Rainbow Gathering took place among the hills, meadows, and forests of the Bridger-Teton National Forest in Western Wyoming. It's about 45 minutes from the only thing close to civilization, a town called Big Piney, whose population I'd estimate at about 550.

The Gathering has always been an annual retreat for hippies, counterculture advocates, and nature lovers. But recently it's begun to draw some of the earthier members of the American rave movement, myself included. In fact, this year the Zippies made the event even more appealing by scheduling one of their parties just adjacent to the Gathering. True to form, they wind up arriving at the site too late to entertain anyone but the stragglers. Nevertheless, at its height, almost 15,000 people are in attendance.

Like a rave, the Rainbow Gathering involves so many sights, sounds, and activities that it's difficult to experience them all. I've been here for five of its scheduled seven days, and I'm far from exhausting it. We live in camps, each of which has its own kitchen serving ever-changing meals. Food is cooked in clay ovens that are constructed from materials gathered on site. There have been group discussions on religion, relationships, philosophy, politics, and issues relative to the Gathering itself. Attendees craft candles, pottery, weavings, and carvings. In an area my friend and I have dubbed the Rainbow Spa and Salon, you have the option of bathing or having your hair washed in solar-heated water. Showers are available, but someone has to hold the hose for you.

Alongside the physical similarities between the Gathering and a standard rave, there's the ever-present rhythm that characterizes them both. It doesn't matter whether it's 40 beats per minute with laser accompaniment, or 10 to 50 flame-lit drummers in the middle of a two-hour, fireside percussion marathon—you develop an intense relationship to the rhythm. At raves, from the moment you arrive until your exhausted departure, you are surrounded by the beat. At the Rainbow Gathering, you fall asleep and wake up to drumming. The universal rhythm is constant.

But there are differences between the Gathering and a rave, especially in the attitude toward technology. Many Rainbow family members take pride in their shunning of the technological advances of contemporary culture. Some consider them aspects of "Babylon," a term they frequently use to disparage modern-day society. While it's certainly admirable to live without relying on the sometimes destructive advances wrought by science and chemistry, it makes me sad to think of the limitations these people could be placing on themselves. Maybe by consciously ignoring the outside world they've managed to achieve an ignorant bliss, but they're also missing out on the limitless possibilities that technology affords, which inspire so much hope in ravers.

Thankfully, most Rainbow Gatherers, whatever their beliefs, are here for a greater purpose. The Gathering is a break in time, an opportunity to enjoy what the earth has to offer outside the world of the manmade. If there's a message here, it's a simple one, and it applies to hippies and ravers alike. We must use modern life to keep these natural spirits alive, and make room for the unknown spirits that await us.

London, England: It's several months later and we're in a London hotel fighting off jet lag's weird high. Maybe we can pick up some pointers from these raver old-timers. Rave was born here. Actually, if you want to get technical about it, rave was probably born in Chicago on the day Genesis P-Orridge of Psychic TV noticed a record-store bin marked "Acid House," and mistakenly thought it meant acid as in LSD—it really meant acid as in the corrosive liquid. Anyway, P-Orridge took a slew of these records home to London, and, when the music wasn't as wild as the tag had implied, he set out to record what he'd heard in his daydreams. This new, tweaked-out, vaguely psychedelic dance music sounded stunning on ecstasy, the drug of choice among trendy young Londoners. And it was extremely influential in both the rock and dance scenes which have been traditionally less separatists than those in the States. When club DJs started adding this new acid house to their play lists, and rock band like Happy Mondays, Stone Roses, and Charlatans ran with the ball, they kick-started a musical genre that would eventually filter overseas and lead people like ourselves starry-eyed to the source.

We'd heard rave was essentially dead in England. As far as we can tell, it is and t isn't. Certainly English rave has gentrified over the last few years. Walking down Camden High Street—a kind of scruffier Melrose—techno blasts from most storefronts. On TV, corporate advertisers like Coca-Cola and Hyundai use it to audio-wrap their products. Even the BBC—establishment central—intros and outros their newscasts with weakling techno instrumentals.

What is all but dead are the large, illegal outdoor events that were British rave culture's early meat and potatoes. The government here is famous for its semi-fascism toward countercultural behavior, and ravers appear to be its current enemy number one. The Criminal Justice Bill, aimed in part at eliminating rave from the landscape, became a law at the end of last year, despite protests and demonstrations. The bill allows police to shut down any public gathering of more than a couple dozen people.

And there are serious problems within the scene itself. just a month before our arrival, a young Scottish raver sold some bad ecstasy and was literally cooked alive on an Edinburgh dance floor, inspiring the hysteria-prone English tabloids to call for a crackdown and instigating a fierce debate within the pages of rave-oriented magazines such as Mixmag (e.g., "Do we need to being self-policing our drug use?").

Chris Campion, a London-based freelance writer, is a friend of a friend of Joel's. One night early in our visit, he offers to guide us through Megatripolis, a weekly indoor rave hosted by Heaven, one of the city's largest dance clubs. Campion, a wiry 25-year-old with big, perpetually spooked brown eyes, is enthusiastic about he music, but—and here he echoes virtually every British rave aficionado we come into contact with—he feels rave is all but spent as a social force in England. He doesn't go out to events much anymore, preferring to hole up at home with his headphones. The last time he set foot in Megatripolis, it was years ago when the crowds were smallish and ultra-hip.

Tonight the club is packed, and there's a decided "bridge and tunnel" non-look to most of the assembled. The dance floors are packed, but the energy is weird. Across one of the rooms is a bar with a thick fringe of thirsty people. Maybe that's the problem. In the States—and this was apparently the case during the early, heady days of English rave—alcohol is considered anathema to the transcendent nature of the rave experience. But now, with the government on rave's tail, and the move to safer quarters indoors...well, pollution was probably inevitable.

Our hopes for English rave are raised later in the week, when, scouring *Time Out,* London's popular weekly entertainment magazine, we notice an ad for something called Megadog. Mega-dog turns out to be a real mind-blower on the order of Narnia and other large stateside events. Set in the sprawling auditorium and courtyard of a disused-looking university complex, it features several different environmentally distinct areas, and a flux of entertainment, from an extraordinary light show to berserk circus acts. This being England, the assembly seems a bit more reserved than we're used to, but there's that same tenable, indefinable feeling of mutual comfort and kindly interactions. Joel suddenly merges with the dancing horde, his face so blissed it's almost unrecognizable.

Dennis watches Joel from the sidelines, then loses sight, and eventually he's just as high on all the beauty as everyone else.

Part of that beauty has to do with the absence of sexual tension. People are sweaty and shirtless. Bodies are moving in ways that would normally inspire, well, hormones. But nobody's cruising, or not that we can pick up on. Maybe it's the drugs. Unlike alcohol or coke. pot and ecstasy do something sweet to the brain that seems to outbalance whatever lust incidentally arises: pot induces self-involvement; ecstasy spins its cocoon of well-being. Everyone at Megadog seems kind of spaced and contentedly alone, despite their proximity. Maybe the asexuality is influenced by techno, which tends to be rather cerebral. Maybe it's a reaction to AIDS. Probably it's all of the above, and more.

Techno doesn't get any more cerebral than the electronic music of the Future Sounds of London. Their 1994 CD, *Lifeforms,* is so far advanced in every way from the work of even their most adventurous peers that it's impossible to characterize in a word. ("Progressive" maybe? Is that term safely disassociated from '70s pomp merchants like Yes and ELP?)

One day near the very end of our visit, we make a pilgrimage to FSOL's recording studio/second home in the north London suburbs, hoping to hear a less embittered read on the current state of rave. Gary Cobain, a stylish intellectual, and Brian Dougans, his painfully shy cohort, respond to our inquiries with a shrug and a very slight mist about the eyes. FSOL's plans have nothing to do with dance events. They talk about wanting to transgress every tradition of the pop music world, and build instead an extremely high-tech relationship between their music and whoever wants to listen. When they perform live, it's here in the studio, linked by telephone lines to an international array of radio stations and concert venues. They're in the early stages of starting their own television station, hoping to reformat their increasingly far-flung sound investigations.

FSOL may be idealists in desperate need of a reality check, or they may have just put their collective finger on a practical way to translate rave's extraordinary goals into cultural realities. Time will tell. In the meantime, they make an amazing noise. Just think, continues Cobain, gesturing wildly, the more the government tries to regulate art production, the more sophisticated FSOLs mode of communication will become. Dancing, drugs, record companies, MTV, governments...artists don't need to be tied down by any of them. "Just fucking imagine it," he enthuses. Joel and Dennis share a glance, and our trip sort of flashes before our eyes. Okay, cool. We can.

King of the Mumble: Stephen Malkmus

DENNIS COOPER: What's your writing process like?
STEPHEN MALKMUS: Well, unfortunately I sometimes feel a little guilty. I know some people... For instance, Robert Pollard of Guided by Voices is writing down stuff all the time. I tried to do that. I went to Malaysia by myself before we recorded *Brighten the Corners,* and I brought my computer, and I tried to write about what was happening there, and about the people I saw, like I guess writers do. But I couldn't really write until we were done with the music.

The music comes first?
I'll have a first line maybe, off the top of my head, and I'll kind of build off that. Usually I'll be thinking of what I've read lately. Like I'd been reading John Ashbery before we did the album. He's brilliant, and I took his work as like, Okay, I can do something like that. It's not against the rules. I don't have to do something that's really formal.

I read that you appropriated lines from Ashbery's "The Tennis Court Oaths."
[laughing] No, no.

I tried to compare your lyrics to the poems, and the only thing I could
find the common was the word 'concierge.'
Mm-hm. That could well be. But I was thinking of *The Tenant,* that Roman Polanski movie too. That always reminds me of a concierge. I love that movie. It's so sick.

I can see the Ashbery connection in the sense that your songs seem personal, but, at the same time, they adopt a kind of omniscient, everyman stance.

That's true. Say in "Type Slowly," the line 'Sherry, you smell different." I was thinking about how if you haven't seen an old girlfriend in a while, she'll still smell the same. People generally smell a recognizable way, even if you haven't seen them in years. I thought it would be strange and sort of disorienting and sad to say, You smell different. I mean, that sounds personal, but it's so distanced, and then the lyrics go off in this sort of...hallucinatory way, I guess.

Do you write in song form, or in paragraphs, or...?

This time we did this thing where I sang the songs right before we mixed them, which is very radical. I don't think bands normally do that. We recorded all the music in North Carolina. Then I had a month before we mixed and sang in which to think about what I wanted to do. I like to give myself a deadline and just hope that something comes out. I have to force myself. So say in "Shady Lane," I had, like, [singing] 'A shady lane, everybody wants one.' And I had the first line. And I had, 'recognize your heirs,' because I just thought it was funny to have to recognize your heirs. Other than that, it was sort of mix-and-match at the last second.

The tones shift pretty intricately in the songs. I assumed they were very carefully composed.

It's hard to say where it comes from. I wanted the album to have a psychedelic edge, and have a hallucinogenic edge, but not have it be acid based. Have it be a little bit weird, and a little bit creepy, but not self-consciously so. For me the third verse is always the big mystery verse. That's always last minute. Because the third verse is, like, Okay, the story's been told. Now we can screw around. Everyone knows it's coming around again, because it's a song. We don't have to bang the dead horse by that point. The war's been won.

Your songs have a lot of room in them. It's almost like the music and the lyrics and the singing are on different planes.

Well, as a point of comparison, Sonic Youth, a band I

love...Thurston tends to sing with the guitar line. For me, it's a battle to think in the fourth dimension—because I'm the guitarist, and sometimes the bass player—to think of how to have that extra person in there, the singer, contributing this additional element.

Do you write, apart from songwriting? I know you're a big reader.

Not that much. I have a pretty protestant, pragmatist thing to my writing. I only do it when I have a goal. I love to read, and be a dumb reader of books, a fan, and think, This is so beautiful, and not compare it to what I do. The thing is, I don't generally like reading books by people my own age, for some reason. I gravitate toward fortysomething men, midlife crisis writers like...um, Barry Hannah and Russell Banks or whoever. I guess I don't think I know enough to write a book. Maybe I should try, though. I could keep a journal.

Don't worry about it. You write great songs.

Yeah. That's enough...isn't it?

Of course.

I don't know...I'm sort of afraid of being a real good vocalist or lyricist. I mean, I try really hard, and when you weigh what's important about a great band, those are crucial things, but...I worry about it.

You used to work at the Whitney Museum in New York, didn't you?

Yeah, Steve West did too. It was sort of an escape for me. Normally I like being idle. But in New York, it's so cold and lonely. I think, like most people, I thought that I needed to have something to do. Anyway, I was a guard. It just basically involved standing against a wall for thirty-five hours a week.

So were you interested in contemporary art? Did you read *Artforum* and all that?

Yeah. I mean, Steve and I were both outsiders there. We were both more into reading and music than art. It was an icing-on-the-cake type of thing. I developed an appreciation for things that I never would have otherwise. Post-minimalist sculpture, you know. Eva Hesse, Barry LeVay, Charles Ray. Humans like to classify and name things. And just for my own satisfaction, it's fun to be able to go to a museum and say, Oh, that's a David Salle. Typical bourgeois thing, you know. 'I know art.' We were guards so we were invisible, and that was nice, especially at openings. It was the end of the 80s. So Ashley Bickerton would be there smoking non-filter cigarettes and being daring. Those kinds of 80s guys were dying at that point, and Bruce Nauman, who I really like, was becoming the intellectual leader for all the younger artists.

Did the bad reaction to *Wowee Zowee* disappoint you a lot?

Not really. It's so blurry to me now. I think about it historically, about what it'll all mean eventually. That's the only way I can stand it. I mean, more people liked it than liked *Trout Mask Replica* when it came out. Not that *Wowee Zowee* is even close to being that kind of work of genius, but I mean in terms of sales and stuff like that.

Every Pavement fan I know, including myself, loved it and were excited by it. We all felt that after *Crooked Rain, Wowee Zowee* was exactly the kind of move we wanted you guys to make. It seemed like a challenge to yourselves and to us.

That's what I thought. It really polarized people. We sent out these bad, muddy advance tapes before it was mastered properly. That might have been part of the problem.

Do you think that things will be different or odder for Pavement in England now, what with you being perceived as the saviours of Blur?

It's hard to tell. We're going there tomorrow. When something like that happens, it just seems really artificial, because it's England, and anything you get from that is going to be so transitory. I think people genuinely like us there. And I just imagine that that guy Damon will move on to another influence next album. That's his style. Blur is all concept anyway. That would be a terrible thing, if that was your only claim to fame. That you influenced Blur.

It could have been worse. It could have been Cast.

[laughing] Totally.

Blur's a clever band. They always make me think that there's more there than meets the ear, and that's all you can really ask of English bands. Whereas Oasis seems so gentrified.

I have a soft spot for Oasis, and that kind of lunkheaded thing. Rock 'n' roll, man. Tunes. And just dumbness. I could never do that. It's like a Beatles-versus-Stones thing. The Beatles are more art-school boys, whereas the Stones were appropriating black music and trying to be rock. I'm more likely to be a Beatle than a Stone, because I just couldn't do that. I guess Jon Spencer would be a Stone.

What are you listening to?

I don't know. I haven't really gotten an informed opinion about new stuff yet. Like Tortoise. I approve of what they're doing. I'm on their side. I'm supportive, but I don't really listen to them in my house. I listen to a lot of jazz. I like noise bands, the absurdity and fun of it, but I mostly love bands that give songs, put the vocals up loud and go for it. It takes more guts to do that. In the end, I'd want to support those bands.

What's the most beautiful place you've ever been?

Well, we did this video shoot yesterday out in the Simi Valley. Very California suburban landscape. It wasn't the kitsch element that I liked. It was the light, the California weather that was relaxing and beautiful to me. The clichéd suburban sprawl. But then I'm the kind of person who loves to defend things that everyone else hates, especially in music. People say, Ugh, the Spice Girls, and I'll say, They're the greatest.

Well, I like Silverchair. What do you say to that?

Silverchair's good. I kind of like Alice in Chains. They have a lot of dumb songs, but they have a spooky psychedelic side that I like. Silverchair has this beautiful mix of that and

'70s music. Their videos are always stupid marketing strategy ones, but I close my eyes, and I think they're cool. Generally bands that a lot of people like, they almost always do have something. There are some exceptions. I think Bush isn't very good.

You can't get much worse than Live.

Yeah, Live. I call them Live as a protest. They've asked us to support them twice, and we were like, No, thank you. Their new song is bad, scary bad. I'm sure it's going to be followed by some earnest ballad. It's funny how bands like Smashing Pumpkins do the same exact pattern for every album. They introduced a hard rocking song for their first single. Then they did "Today" and "1979" respectively, which I think are their best songs. And then came the string ballad. It works. Smashing Pumpkins... More like Smashing Marketing Plan.

You mentioned the video shoot. Spike Jonze was the director, right?

Yeah. It's for "Shady Lane." It's bordering on *Logan's Run* meets Todd Haynes' *Safe*. We're out in this valley that's very antiseptic, and wearing all these color cottons, and we're kind of zoned. I could do that pretty well, because when I was younger my parents were into EST and stuff. They weren't into crystals or anything. It's pretty bourgeois New Age style, what they did. But they got touched by it.

You live in Portland now. Why?

My parents live in Sun Valley, the ski resort near there. And they'd had all my furniture since I moved east in 1990. Anyway, I moved to Portland partially because I'd split up with a girlfriend, and I wanted to start over. I wanted to go to the West Coast. I couldn't live in San Francisco because I was born near there, and that would be too much. To move to L.A. would be too audacious a step. And Seattle kind of sucks. The people there are so mean. Portland's nice, low key. It's kind of small. I think I might move back to New York though. I have friends there. You make your best friends in your twenties, I think. I thought I could start over and make new friends, but you get kind of set in your ways. The guys in Pavement are my best friends, and they're all out East basically.

Will you miss the West Coast?

Sure. It's so much more beautiful out here, the weather, the light, and it's so stunning visually. But the lack of history thing... it's all relative, but geologic time here is so intense, plates always moving, earthquakes. I guess I just want the comfort of New York's history, such as it is.

You guys are on the road a lot. Any interesting tour stories?

Well, Keanu Reeves came to our show in New York. He gave us a book on chess. He said, 'I heard you're chess fans.' He was really nervous and shy. A friend of mine saw him in a restaurant by himself the other day. It seemed kind of sad. Keanu eating by himself in a mid-scale restaurant on the Sunset Strip. Poor little guy.

Yeah, since he's put on weight, nobody likes him anymore.

I know. What's up with that?

Beats me. Okay, one last question. It's an odd one, but go with it, and I'll explain why I asked it in a second. Name your three favorite animals.

Hm. I'd pick a bird for my first choice, some sort of predator. A falcon or a hawk, because it seems like a pretty good life. Except killing little creatures would bum me out, I guess. Second, I think I'd go land. My land creature would be...maybe a lynx or a mountain lion. I'd want to be on top of the food chain. Lone creature, an outsider cruising around. Fast. Can't be fucked with. Third...well, I should pick something warm and open and loving. How about a nice otter, cracking clam shells, having fun, making children laugh.

Well, that was a psychological test question. There's some official validation for it in psychiatric circles. The first animal represents who you want to be. The sec-

ond represents who you are. And the third represents what you want in a lover.

That's nice. That works really well. Yeah, I would like to be with the otter.

Beauty and Sadness

River Phoenix's death has startled and depressed everyone I know, even people who had previously dismissed movie stardom as a form of corporate-induced mass hypnosis. About 72 hours after his fatal collapse, a cynical friend and I happened on a recent television interview in which the earnest young actor was laying out his future plans, and we burst into horrified tears. Weird. That's what we keep saying: Weird that he's dead; weird that we care so much. Phoenix seems to have been admired by a whole lot of people in relative secrecy—an artist whose work insinuated itself into viewers' good graces, no matter how faltering it particular vehicle, nor how initially cold-hearted his audience. To wit: As I write this, *Hard Copy,* hardly a show known for its moral fortitude, is heaping praise on a paparazzi photographer who couldn't bring himself to document the actor's dying convulsions.

The word on the streets, even in the gossip columns, had always had Phoenix living a pretty honorable and pristine existence relative to the goings-on of his peers—a poetry-reading, vegetarian, open-minded, Democratic life, free of Shannen Doherty's creepiness, Judd Nelson's self-destructiveness, Mickey Rourke's bombast. Occasionally you'd hear about him standing tensely and unsociably on the fringe of some art gallery opening: S/M performer Bob Flanagan, once a member of the improvisational comedy troupe the Groundlings, remembers Phoenix staggering drunkenly onto the stage during one their skits. But big deal. He was a *kid.* Mostly he seemed, if anything, too serious, too incapable of relaxing into a benign mindlessness, even for a minute. In a recent issue of *Detour* magazine, he positively excoriated many of his fellow actors for being ego-driven, and spoke of wanting to move not just out of L.A., but out of this wretched country entirely. Nonetheless, he did continue to live here, and he did die under the influence of drugs at a trendy local nightspot. So it's hard to know what to think right now.

Death always focuses people, even if the demystification process takes years in some cases. It shouldn't with Phoenix, since his sincerity and forthrightness have never been in question. Ultimately, barring unforeseen revelations, his name, his work, will acquire that particular cult holiness that people naturally create to fill in the blanks around the prematurely taken. Phoenix will be our James Dean, just like so many pundits are predicting. Meanwhile, by default, his fellow "outsider" types like Keanu Reeves, Matt Dillon, et al., are stuck being our Marlon Brando, if they're lucky. And that's because actors can't compete with their fans' imaginations, and the accomplishments we'll fantasize for a hypothetical mature Phoenix can't help but outstrip the potential feats of the bona fide middle-aged Phoenix. Life's funny, and even a little disgusting, that way.

Comparisons between Phoenix and James Dean are lazy, not to mention ubiquitous at this point, though they did share several of the qualities that separate great actors from mere signifiers of glamour. Both were extremely attentive to detail yet seemingly incapable of submerging their actual emotions under an artificial personality. No matter how peripheral Phoenix's role—the scatterbrained junior hippie in *I Love You to Death,* the poet/Casanova in *The Life and Times of Jimmy Reardon,* the loyal spooked son of Harrison Ford's megalomaniac in *The Mosquito Coast*—he was always a little more perceptive and soulful—more real—than anyone else onscreen. Even in as offbeat and dislocated a milieu as the Portland street-hustler scene of *My Own Private Idaho,* Phoenix's Mike stood out as unusually lonesome—someone who was afraid of, and simultaneously astonished by, his squalid conditions, who desperately sought affection from others while at the same time avoiding sympathizers like the plague. It was a performance that, like most of Dean's, seemed to distill the confused melancholy of an emerging generation.

Phoenix was the son of hippie parents. He sometimes described his acting style as an attempt to represent how he felt upon trading his family's blanket humanism for the film industry's hatred of the unrepentant individual. Actress/performer Ann Magnuson, who co-starred with Phoenix in *Jimmy Reardon,* once remarked to me with a kind of amazement how solid and unspoiled he seemed even then, in the teen-idol phase of his career. As someone who entered showbiz with her own mixed feelings, she wondered how or even *if* he'd survive its multifarious forms of corruption. Maybe that very struggle explains why, as he aged, his performances exuded ever more sadness and pointed discomfort. His best recent work found him playing overgrown kids who clung for this lives to youthful notions of a perfect romantic and/or familial love.

In a profession that divides it young into marginalized wackos with integrity like Crispin Glover and John Lurie, or hipster sellouts like Christian Slater and Robert Downey, Jr., Phoenix was that once-in-a-decade actor honest enough to connect powerfully with people his own age, and skillful enough to remind members of an older generation of the intensity they'd lost.

Grain of the Voice

In John Lydon's autobiography, *Rotten: No Irish, No Blacks, No Dogs,* he compares Nirvana to Eddie and the Hot Rods, a late-'70s R&B bar band who'd lucked into a little popularity and acclaim during the dawn of British punk, when any group with short hair and short songs were temporarily mistaken for revolutionaries. "It really annoys me," Lydon writes, "...when [Nirvana] say they were influenced by the Sex Pistols. They clearly can't be. They missed the point somewhere." My first thought on reading this passage was Jesus, what a clueless fool. But thinking more about it, I realized he had a point, however reductive and however inadvertently self-indicting.

Lydon, who likes to characterize himself as a talented troublemaker, can't see Nirvana for the darkness and length of his own shadow. To him, the members of Nirvana can only be proteges, and so their very admiration of his work becomes an embarrassment, an admission of weakness. A classic pre-feminist bully, Lydon all but calls them fags and wussies. But of course, the very qualities that made him and other punk hardliners suspicious of Nirvana—sincerity, overemotionalism, formal conservatism, intellectual spazziness—are at the center of why they're a great band.

The Sex Pistols predated AIDS, homelessness, MTV. Not to say life was easy in the mid-'70s, but Nirvana didn't have the luxury, nor the megalomaniacal naïvete, to attempt a coup of popular culture. In this world, it's hard enough just to get an absolutely honest song on the airwaves. Nirvana, like most interesting current bands, just wanted to represent their exact feelings appropriately. Luckily, in their case, they were guided by Kurt Cobain, a gifted if obviously tormented man with high ideals, original ideas, and a beautifully erratic way of expressing himself.

Kurt Cobain may have loved John Lydon, but I suspect that it was in the way a kid loves his or her abusive father. Unlike that cynical old fuck, Cobain wasn't a monster, ever. At his worst, he was a mess, but so are most of us, only we get to act out our shit among friends, and not in front of people who think our every woe is a generational signifier. I mean, Cobain's idea of media manipulation was to wear a Daniel Johnston T-shirt during photo sessions. He may have been rich, but he thought like an anarchist. He wanted to share. He wrote consistently great lyrics about not being able to express himself adequately, he sang like God with a dog's mouth, and he believed in the communicative powers of popular music. And precisely because he believed, Nirvana wound up doing what the Pistols could only masturbate thinking about.

Cobain's work nailed how a ton of people feel. There are few moments in rock as bewilderingly moving as when he mumbled, "I found it hard/It's hard to find/Oh well, whatever/Nevermind." There's that bizarre, agonized, and devastating promise he keeps making throughout Heart-Shaped Box": "Wish that I could eat your cancer when you turn black." Take a look in his eyes the next time MTV runs the "Heart-Shaped Box" video, and see if you can sort out the pain from the ironic detachment from the horror from the defensiveness.

American culture has reached a strange impasse, which is largely the fault of our pathetic educational system. It's left us intellectually undernourished, emotionally confused, and way, way too vulnerable. That imbalance may have produced artists like Cobain, but it has also softened our brains to the point where we just let political and corporate higher-ups of various sorts manipulate our very ways of receiving information. Instead of being encouraged to expand imaginatively on the music we listen to, we're told to reduce everything in our world into simple rights and wrongs, effectives and ineffectives, yeses and nos. We comply because the world is scary and because we understandably want to be coddled by the things that interest us. Kurt Cobain, so conflicted in his attitude toward success, and so complex in his ideas about love and politics, was a classic beneficiary and victim of this dilemma.

What's amazing is that after all that interference, he won. Well, he didn't, but Nirvana did. Nirvana, a band that embodied every important quality that punk had ever championed managed for a brief period to flip off power-mongers and signal believers with the very same gesture. And, in succeeding so spectacularly, and so cleanly, Cobain and crew showed what was possible, even in this ugly and demoralized culture. Unfortunately, with his stupid, infuriating death, he also showed us what our belief costs.

Flanagan's Wake

Bob Flanagan and I met in the late '70s. At the time he'd published one thin book of gentle, Charles Bukowski–influenced poetry entitled *The Kid Is the Man* (Bombshelter Press, 1978). We were both in our mid 20s, born less than a month apart. I was sporting a modified punk/bohemian look and hated all things hippie-esque. Bob looked like one of the Allman Brothers: thin, junkie pale, with shoulder-length hair, a handlebar mustache, and an ever-present acoustic guitar that he'd occasionally strum while belting out parodies of Bob Dylan songs. His style put me off initially, as mine did him, but I found his poetry amusing, edgy, and odd, and his clown-ish, sarcastic personality belied a deeply submissive nature.

There was a new, upstart literary community forming around Los Angeles' Beyond Baroque Center, where Bob was leading a poetry workshop. I had met the poet Amy Gerstler in college, and she and I began to hang out at Beyond Baroque in hopes of meeting other young writers. After a few months of hunting and pecking through the crowds, a small, tight gang of us had begun to form, including, in addition to Bob, Amy, and myself, the poets Jack Skelley, David Trinidad, Kim Rosenfield, and Ed Smith, artist/fiction writer Benjamin Weissman, and a number of other artists, filmmakers, and the like. We partied together, showed one another our works-in-progress, and generally caused a ruckus in the then-dormant local arts scene.

Very early on, Bob told us he had cystic fibrosis, and that it was an incurable disease that would probably kill him in his early 30s—if he were lucky. But apart from his scrawniness, his persistent and terrible cough, and the high-protein liquids he constantly drank to keep his weight up, he was, if anything, the most energetic and pointedly reckless of us all. At that stage, Bob's poetry only obliquely described his illness, and barely touched on his masochistic sexual tendencies. In fact, it took him a while to reveal the details of his sex life to his new chums. I think the fact that my work dealt explicitly with my own rather dark sexual fantasies made it relatively easy in my case, and I remember his surprise and relief when I responded to his confession with wide-eyed fascination.

Bob was working on the densely lyrical, mock-humanist poems that would later be collected in his second book, *The Wedding of Everything* (Sherwood Press, 1983). He began to encode within his poetry little clues and carefully offhand references to S/M practices, and gradually, as his vocabulary became more direct, the sex, and in particular his unabashed enjoyment of submission, humiliation, and pain, were revealed as the true subjects of his work.

Writing was difficult for Bob. One, he was a perfectionist. Two, with his sexual preferences finally out in the open, he was more interested in talking about and enacting fantasies that had already played themselves out in daydreams and in private autoerotic practices. It was around this time that Bob met Sheree Levin, aka Sheree Rose, a housewife turned punk scenester with a master's degree in psychology. They fell in love, and, profoundly influenced both by her feminism and her interest in Wilhelm Reich's notions of "body therapy," Bob changed his work instantaneously and radically. For the rest of his life, Bob, usually working in collaboration with Sheree, used his writing, art, video, and performance works to chronicle their relationship with Rimbaudian lyricism and abandon.

Bob began to live part-time at Sheree's house in West Los Angeles, along with her two kids, Matthew and Jennifer. Bob was an exhibitionist, and Sheree loved to shock people, so their rampant sexual experimentation became very much a public spectacle. It wasn't unusual to drop by and find the place full of writers, artists, and people from the S/M community, all flying on acid and/or speed, Bob naked and happily enacting orders from the leather-clad Sheree. During this period Bob published two books, *Slave Sonnets* (Cold Calm Press, 1986) and the notorious *Fuck Journal* (Hanuman Books, 1987). He also began an ambitious book-length prose poem called *The Book of Medicine,* which he hoped would explore the relationship between his illness and his fascination with pain. At his death, the work remained incomplete, though sections had been used in his performances and have appeared in anthologies.

I was programming events at Beyond Baroque in those days and, as we were all interested in performance art, I organized a night called "Poets in Performance," in which we tried our hands at the medium. Bob and Sheree's piece involved Bob, clad only in a leather mask, improvising poetry while Sheree pelted him with every imaginable food item. It was such a hit, and Bob was so thrilled by this successful merging of his fetishes, his art, and his exhibitionist tendencies, that he and Sheree began doing similar, increasingly extreme performances around town. Perhaps the most famous and influential of thee works, *Nailed,* 1989, began with a gory slide show by Rose and concluded, after various, highly stylized S/M acts, with Bob nailing his penis to a wooden board. The performance made Bob infamous, and he was subsequently asked to perform in rock videos by Nine Inch Nails, Danzig, and Godflesh, as well as being offered a role in Michael Tolkin's film *The New Age. Nailed* also interested Mike Kelley, who later used Bob and Sheree as models in one of his pieces and wound up doing several collaborations with the duo.

Coincidentally, interest in S/M and body modification

was growing in youth culture, especially after the publication of *Modern Primitives* (RE/Search), which profiled Sheree's life as a dominatrix. Bob was a hero and model to the denizens of this subculture, even as he found much of their interest to be superficial and trendy. Bob was always and only an artist. He never cloaked his masochism in pretentious symbolism, nor did he use his work to perpetuate the fashionable idea that S/M is a new, pagan religious practice. His performances, while exceedingly graphic and visceral, involved a highly estheticized, personal, pragmatic challenge to accepted notions of violence, illness, and death. For all the obsessive specificity of his interests, Bob was a complex man who wanted simultaneously to be Andy Kaufman, Houdini, David Letterman, John Keats, and a character out of a de Sade novel. So his performances were as wacky and endearing as they were disturbing and moving. For example, at the same time he was making a name for himself as a shockmeister, he was performing on Sundays with improvisational comedy troupe The Groundlings, in hopes of fulfilling his lifelong ambition to be a stand-up comedian.

By the early '90s, Bob's physical condition was worsening. He was having to hospitalize himself before and after performances just to get through them. He and Sheree proposed a performance/installation piece to the Santa Monica Museum of Art, which was accepted and became *Visiting Hours,* a multimedia presentation comprising sculpture, video, photography, text, and Bob himself poised in a hospital bed acting as the work's amiable host and information center. *Visiting Hours* was popular and critically well-received, eventually traveling to the New Museum in new York and the School of the Museum of Fine Arts in Boston. In 1993, RE/Search published *Supermasochist,* a book entirely devoted to Bob's life and work. Also that year, filmmaker Kirby Dick began to shoot a feature-length documentary film about Bob and Sheree entitled *Sick,* which will be released this fall.

There was some hope during this period that Bob might be able to have a lifesaving heart and lung transplant, but, after months of tests it was determined that his lungs has deteriorated too much to allow him to survive the operation, and he began to accept that he had maybe a year yet to live. He and Sheree concentrated on visual art pieces, some of which were exhibited at Galerie Analix in Geneva and at NGBK Gallery in Berlin. The duo collaborated on a last installation work, *Dust to Dust,* which Sheree is currently completing, and Bob kept a year-long diary of his physical deterioration, *Pain Journal,* which will be published in the future. Even as most of Bob's life began to be taken up with stints in the hospital and painful physical therapy, he was still on the scene, frail but good-natured, using his omnipresent oxygen tank as a comical prop just as he had once used his acoustic guitar. Right after Christmas, Bob went into the hospital one final time and died on January 4, 1996. In the 15 years I knew him, Bob grew from a minor poet into a unique and profoundly original artist who accomplished more than he ever imagined he could, and whose loss, predictable or not, is one of the greatest difficulties those of us who knew and loved him have ever had to face.

KING JUNK

Why is the death of William Burroughs such a curiously uneventful event? Despite a superficial resemblance to his friend Allen Ginsberg's recent passing, the two deaths couldn't feel more different. Like Burroughs, Ginsberg was both a writer well past his prime and a spotlight addict inclined to interlope on passing youth cultural movements as a way to life-extend his legend. Nonetheless, Ginsberg remained a force to the end, an artist with a sincere political and spiritual agenda who saw his fame as a way to effect cultural change. His presence never stopped mattering to some faction of society, however small their number or offbeat their cause. His death was a surprisingly powerful blow, even to people who'd long since turned their attentions away from his poetry in embarrassment.

Burroughs, on the other hand, was essentially an active relic who had exploited the mystique around his early work for so long that I suspect even he didn't know why he was famous anymore. While he continued to write, he was less an artist than a retiree who dabbled at his former craft. Despite the omnipresence of his name, he himself had ceased to participate in our world decades ago. He was an old man living quietly in the middle of nowhere, invisible apart from the occasional cameo, attached to us only by that famous visage and voice, and by the patented anecdotes and crackpot theories that he respun endlessly for any interviewer willing to make the trek to Kansas. The Burroughs whom most of us know and love is an echo, and, thanks to the miracles of sampling, that echo will continue unimpeded for as long as there are young rebels in need of a transgressive figurehead.

In a way, Burroughs died in the late 70s when he was resurrected from relative obscurity, and repackaged as a kind of outlaw comedian/philosopher. Victor Bockris' influential 1981 book, *In the Bunker With William Burroughs,* a collection of transcribed dinner conversations and photos, presents him as a cranky, befuddled living legend who, when not putting on clownish displays of outre behavior, was propped up in front of a passing array of rock stars who seemingly meant nothing to him. It's a well known secret that beginning with his "comeback" novel *Cities of the Red Night* (1981). Burroughs' prose was a product of partial ghostwriting, and that his involvement in his books diminished steadily to the point where there seemed to be nothing but textual smoke and mirrors anymore. Perhaps this is not a bad thing in and of itself, as he was an amusing character to have around, and everybody's got to pay the rent somehow, but the result is that his death feels almost completely abstract. The effect on me, and on most of the people I've spoken to in the last few days, is a kind of cold fascination to see what his work will look like once the atmosphere around it has cleared of marketing shenanigans.

Don't get me wrong, Burroughs was an important figure, but for several specific reasons. He perfected (though did not in fact invent) the cut-up technique, one of the touchstones of postmodernism, and an influence on innumerable writers, artists, and filmmakers, not to mention most of the important rock/electronic bands since the 60s. He accidentally popularized the idea of experimental writing by being such a presentable, grandfatherly kook that people bought his novels because they were amused by his personal style. Before heroin addiction stunted his talent, Burroughs wrote a handful of brilliant novels, basically everything from *Naked Lunch* (1959) to *The Wild Boys* (1969). Along with Jean Genet, John Rechy, and Ginsberg, he helped make homosexuality seem cool and highbrow, providing gay liberation with a delicious edge. Those were his gifts to contemporary culture, and they are not insubstantial. The rest of the Burroughs mystique—the gun toting, the belief in UFOs, ghosts, and elaborate CIA conspiracies, the cheerleading for heroin—was pure showbiz. Not that he didn't actually love dangerous weapons, do drugs into his 80s, and sit in Orgone Boxes daydreaming of enlightenment, but the mythic status of those oddball personal habits had everything to do with the contexts in which they were placed.

Gus Van Sant, in whom Burroughs found and unusually thoughtful and sympathetic collaborator, is the exception. But to most of the plethora of rock bands, filmmakers, and advertisers who dropped Burroughs' trademark exterior into their product, he was a signifier of their own daring, and little else. And in allowing this indiscriminate dispersal of his image, Burroughs the artist became Burroughs the simplistic and rather meaningless icon, less a living breathing figure than a detachable touchstone of any wild kid's notion of dangerous intelligence. So is it any surprise that his death seems to bear more relationship to the retiring of Joe Camel than it does to, say, the loss of a valuable cultural presence like Ginsberg?

I suspect it will be years before those of us who didn't know Burroughs personally know what we're missing. At the moment, his death mostly raises the possibility that a lot of longstanding questions about him might finally get honest answers. Like was he really a genius or just a very clever concocter of literary hocus pocus? Why did he allow himself to become the poster boy for junkiedom when heroin addiction had decimated his talent and killed slews of his friends and fans? Did he really think, as he was often quoted as saying, that women were an inferior species that should be wiped off the earth? And, more importantly, why didn't more people call him on shit like that? What does it mean that he got away with the manslaughter killing of his wife? Until these and other questions are resolved, Burroughs himself, and by extension his work, will continue to be hidden behind the walking-talking logo who may or may not have died last Saturday.